Flannery O'Connor

A Proper Scaring

Jill P. Baumgaertner

Harold Shaw Publishers
Wheaton, Illinois

*For my husband, Martin,
and my children, Martin and Anna*

Scripture verses are taken from the *King James Version* of the Bible unless otherwise noted.

Grateful acknowledgment is made to Georgia College, Milledgeville, Georgia, for permission to use Flannery O'Connor portraits, photographs, and cartoons from the Ina Dillard Russell Library.

Printed in the United States of America.

Cover photo © 1988 by Tim Vacula is of the carpet in the Flannery O'Connor room at Georgia College.

ISBN 0-87788-272-X

Library of Congress Cataloging-in-Publication Data

Baumgaertner, Jill P.
   Flannery O'Connor.

   (Wheaton literary series)
   Bibliography: p.
   Includes index.
   1. O'Connor, Flannery—Criticism and interpretations.
I. Title.   II. Series.
PS3565.C57Z584   1988   813'.54   87-32346
ISBN 0-87788-272-X

---

97   96   95   94   93   92   91   90   89   88

10   9   8   7   6   5   4   3   2   1

Contents

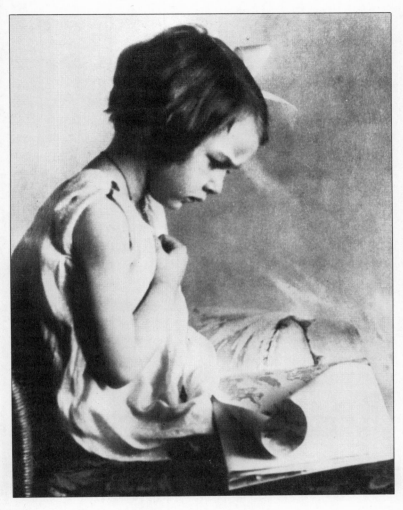

Flannery O'Connor at age three in 1928

*O'Connor Collection, Ina Dillard Russell Library, Georgia College, Milledgeville,
Georgia*

Foreword

I came to Flannery O'Connor late, not until fifteen years or more after her death. I was often told I should read her because like me she was, Heaven help us, a *religious* writer. People who read her also sometimes read me. I even came across occasional articles which touched on us both. We worked the same territory. And that was just the trouble, of course. It's hard enough to work a territory under the best of circumstances, let alone with one eye cocked on somebody else working it in the next cotton patch. Was she doing it better than I was? In what ways was she doing it differently? Did she approach things, see things, feel things at all as I did, especially religious things? Whatever the answers were, I didn't want to know them. I didn't want to be distracted or deflected. I didn't want to be threatened. I just wanted to keep on working my own little plot. And then one day, I forget just how or why, I read her story "A Good Man Is Hard to Find."

I can still remember the impact of it: the killing comedy of the family taking off on its jaunt with the children squabbling in the back seat, the beleaguered father, the loquacious grandmother with her "big black valise that looked like the head of a hippopotamus," and then suddenly the appearance of the scholarly-looking Misfit in his silver-rimmed spectacles and long, creased face, his tan and white shoes with no socks. Except perhaps for Shirley Jackson's "The Lottery," I know of no story by anybody that so devastatingly catches you off guard although needless to say, you are given every reason to be on guard right from the start if you have your wits about you. I knew immediately that she was a wonder, an original. There could be no doubt about that. She was no threat to me or anybody else because her corner of the territory was one that no other writer in Christendom either could possibly work or as far as I know has ever worked, and because it is impossible to imagine her choosing to work any other. From that story on I was hooked, not just by the stories themselves, but by the whole tragicomic red-clay world they come out of and that so richly comes out of them—the fierce old men, the impossible old women and their doomed sons, the ancient children, the odd-balls, the crazy, tormented saints, and always, always, the wild, ragged figure of Jesus moving from tree to tree in the back not only of Hazel Motes's mind but of every tale this extraordinary and Christ-possessed woman ever wrote. Jill Baumgaertner's skill in helping us to see this dimension of her art in particular is one of many reasons to rejoice in this present volume.

"That belief in Christ is to some a matter of life and death has been a stumbling block for readers who would prefer to think of it as a matter of no great consequence," Flannery O'Connor wrote in a note to the second edition of *Wise Blood*. The wonder of it is that even among those readers her reputation stands high. Intellectuals who otherwise steer a very wide berth indeed around religion claim her as their own. She is admired by people as ignorant of Christian thought as Eudora Welty claimed to be in an interview where she said it was only her enthusiasm for O'Connor that led her to look up what the concept of grace was all about. The reason for her popularity in such circles is not hard to find. Perhaps most of all it has to do with the way she writes. Her taut, strong, relentlessly aimed style with all its concreteness and vividness is about as far as you can get from the overripe banalities usually associated with literary piety. And so, of course, is her wit. I suppose it is precisely because she has a mystic's sense of what holiness truly is that she is able to depict in such a wry and sometimes uproarious way the freakish distortions that it suffers at the hands of a mad world. Her laughter comes from a very deep and holy place inside herself, in other words, and that is probably why it is so deeply infectious, why the comic element of her work is not merely one of its embellishments but of its very substance, as inseparable from the tragic element as grace is from sin. In addition to everything else she is surely one of the most profoundly *funny* writers this century has yet produced. Anybody who doubts that has only to read "The Enduring Chill," for instance, where the baby-faced doctor, the unlettered Jesuit, and the two feckless blacks bring to young Asbury, who is alone in believing that he is on his deathbed, exactly what he wants least and, if his soul is to be saved, exactly what he needs most.

If God is to save souls, he must do so with people who for the most part fight tooth and nail against the process. Hazel Motes ends up a saint in spite of himself. Francis Marion Tarwater does everything he can to avoid becoming the prophet he is destined to be. Human life is so distorted and distorting that the grace of God is broken to pieces by it like light through a prism and reaches us looking like everything except what it is. The plaster figure of a Negro with one eye chipped white and holding a piece of plaster watermelon. An old woman who has just had a stroke lurching down the city pavement with her hair undone on one side. It is often through such outlandish means as these that we are to be saved if we are to be saved at all, and opposed to our saving is all the madness and perversity not only of the world we inhabit but of the worlds we carry around inside our skins, that inhabit us. That is the territory that Flannery O'Connor works, and story by story, novel by novel, Dr. Baumgaertner leads us through it with sensitivity, clarity, and a knowledgeability, theological as well as literary, that in spite of its erudition never causes us to lose sight of O'Connor herself in all her living warmth and humanity.

In the index to O'Connor's collected letters, *The Habit of Being*, there is one reference to me as I remember it which says something to the effect that she never read anything by Frederick Buechner. Ah well. And what would she have thought of me if she had? Would she have found my books in any way to her liking, I wonder? Would she at least have recognized me as a fellow worker in the vineyard? Might we conceivably have become friends?

My wife and I detoured through Milledgeville on our drive north from Florida last winter. A helpful woman in charge of the library there told us where she was buried. The cemetery is called Memory Hill, and I could imagine just the kind of smile that must have elicited from her. I asked a black man working around the place if he could possibly direct us to the grave of somebody named Flannery O'Connor. He did it so readily that I asked him if other people came looking for it sometimes. About one or two a day he said. And there it was next to her father's, her birth date just one year earlier than mine, her death date going on twenty-five years ago.

From there, following the librarian's instructions, we drove past the church where she worshiped and on out to Andalusia. We were leery about driving up the dirt road that leads to it from the highway, but there were no signs of life as far as we could see so we did it anyway. There were some cedar trees about, and I assumed that one of them was the one where Robert Fitzgerald tells us her peacocks were given to roosting at night, turning the grass beneath it white with their droppings. The house looked deserted, a medium-sized white farmhouse with a screen porch in front. I snapped a photograph of it. Nothing looks emptier than a house that is empty. Standing there in the spring afternoon, I said some sort of a silent prayer for her. I wished of all things grace to her, of course, and peace. And I said the best I could by way of thanks—to the Lord and giver of Life for giving us her, to her for giving us a glimpse through all the proper scariness and sadness of things down toward the glowing heart.

Frederick Buechner

Preface

I was always surprised that the best garden I ever grew came from Georgia clay. I understand that geologists consider the soil in that region nutrient-poor. But behind a small frame house in Decatur I grew fruit and vegetables I have never been able to duplicate even in soil-rich Illinois.

It was also in college in Georgia that I first encountered Faulkner. In an un-airconditioned dormitory room with crickets already going strong at eight a.m., I read *Absalom! Absalom!* and my life was changed forever. Up to that point literature had been merely diversion for me. With Faulkner I saw literature's true nature. I began to understand that fiction, well-written, in the hands of genius, was truth. I switched majors from chemistry to English. My father had apoplexy.

He should have seen it coming, however. With a list of old addresses that could belong only to a migrant worker or a military family, I had always yearned for a place. (I now occasionally wonder what has happened to all my old addresses, most of which are a gentle blur in my memory.) It was in Faulkner that I discovered both my vocation and rediscovered my place. He reminded me that my strongest early memories were from

Alexandria, Macon, Valdosta, and Montgomery. Any roots I had were Southern. That red Georgia clay seeps into shoes and discolors socks and toes. I am sure it coats the Georgian's lungs. It probably drifts into the crevices of the brain where it sticks. Permanently.

A few years ago I discovered Flannery O'Connor. At the time I was working in an area far afield from the South and its literature. I was doing research for a dissertation on the seventeenth-century poet, John Donne. In the evenings, however, I would purposely read literature from other epochs, and one night I reached for a collection of O'Connor's short stories. I had taught a couple of them in freshman writing classes, but I must not have been ready for them at the time. When I was ready for her (and in many ways John Donne's exaggerated conceits prepared me for her), she stunned me. Who was this violently comic writer? How could prose simultaneously make me laugh and scare me so deeply?

She was a young woman, a Southerner, a Catholic. She was single and lived with her mother until her early death. Her background sounds inauspicious at first, but her influence has been extraordinarily far-reaching. One wonders just how O'Connor's prose could be translated, but it has been—into a dozen languages. During the summer of 1984 the first international conference on Flannery O'Connor was held in Odense, Denmark. Scholars from ten countries spoke. In an age of unbelief, O'Connor's fiction of revelation has found a remarkably strong and broad audience.

Jill P. Baumgaertner

Acknowledgments

Many people have helped me bring this book to publication. The Alumni Office and the staff of the Ina Dillard Russell Library and the Flannery O'Connor Room of Georgia College have been most helpful and gracious to me. I especially appreciate the assistance of Nancy Davis Bray, Special Collections Associate. For their hospitality, good conversation, and the privileged glimpses they afforded me of O'Connor's home territory I thank Louise Hardeman Abbot and W. Louise Florencourt. Thanks are due also to the Alumni Association and the English Department of Wheaton College for grants, encouragement, and support. I particularly want to extend my appreciation for advice about the direction of the book to Professor E. Beatrice Batson, Chair of the English Department during the time I was involved in this project. The unfailing encouragement of Luci Shaw and the kindness of Ramona Cramer Tucker of Harold Shaw Publishers have helped me to complete the book in the time and the shape I had hoped for. Martin Baumgaertner and Jill Pelaez have been most helpful readers of the manuscript through all of its various stages.

Portions of the first chapter have appeared in *The Christian Century* (December 23-30, 1987), and I express my gratitude to the editors for permission to reprint.

___ 1 ___

"The Meaning Is in You":
Flannery O'Connor's Letters

Three weeks *before her death at the age of 39, Flannery O'Connor* copied out a prayer to Saint Raphael and sent it to a woman she had never met, but one who had in the short year and a half of their correspondence become a close friend. This prayer, which O'Connor said she prayed every day, ends with an image of heaven as a home "beyond the region of thunder, in a land that is always peaceful, always serene and bright with the resplendent glory of God." It was also to this woman, Janet McKane, that O'Connor wrote of receiving Communion and the Sacrament of the Sick (formerly known as extreme unction). Flannery O'Connor knew she was dying. In fact, she had lived with this knowledge for thirteen years, ever since she had received the diagnosis of lupus erythematosus, the disease that had killed her father.

It is tempting to speculate about what O'Connor could have accomplished had she lived longer. Fifteen months before her death she wrote: "I appreciate and need your prayers. I've been writing eighteen years and I've reached the point where I can't do again what I know I can do well, and the larger things that I need to do now, I doubt my capacity for doing."[1] Though O'Connor felt this uncertainty about what lay ahead for her as a writer, she also revealed a sense of artistic completion. That she would ask for prayers also indicates a certain measure of anxiety as she approached the unknown. Flannery O'Connor was, after all, not only an artist and a woman of profound faith, she was human in her reluctance to leave what she loved so well. In one of her final letters to Janet McKane, O'Connor quoted Hopkins' lines:

> Márgarét, are you gríeving
> Over Goldengrove unleaving? . . .[2]

Without complaining, she felt a natural human grief. As she had written in an earlier letter, "You have to cherish the world at the same time you struggle to endure it."[3]

For her, writing and faith were life itself and were tightly bound to one another. She identified "conversion," that is, a "character's changing," as the only real subject of good literature,[4] and one can see in her work that what creates story, what creates the necessary conflict, is a character's resistance to God's grace, often leading violently to sudden revelation. In another letter she wrote that loss is often a precondition to conversion. Perhaps it was the loss of her father and her own debilitating illness that helped keep her own faith strong and her writing persistent. She wrote in 1956 that "in a sense sickness is a place, more instructive than a long trip to Europe, and it's always a place where there's no company, where nobody can follow. Sickness before death is a very appropriate thing and I think those who don't have it miss one of God's mercies."[5]

Flannery O'Connor's letters bring into clearer focus the human being behind the art. The O'Connors did not install a telephone at their farm until late in Flannery's life, so in order to communicate with her friends, she wrote to them, and her letters, compiled and edited by her friend Sally Fitzgerald, allow more than just brief glimpses of O'Connor's life. These letters form a diary beginning in 1948 after her graduation from the University of Iowa's School for Writers until her death in 1964. They allow the occasional reader to dip in and out quickly, but they reward the cover-to-cover reader with a strong sense of immediacy. The O'Connor farm, the Georgia characters O'Connor lived with every day, the animals she raised, the visitors who were so often invited to stay for dinner, live as vividly in her letters as they do in her fiction. One is able to see connections between inhabitants of her daily life and characters in her stories. One can watch the genesis and development of her work as she related its progress to her friends, who included not only her literary agent and editors, but also people like Janet McKane whom Flannery never met face-to-face. Her humor reveals itself not only in the anecdote and the punch line, but also in the turn of phrase she used to berate a friend's slip into Freudian terminology or her answer to a professor of English who asked what she considered unreasonable questions.

In addition, O'Connor gave practical advice to her literary friends—not only on work they sent her to read, but also on how to approach writing on a day-to-day basis. These letters also indicate O'Connor's extensive reading, in her requests for books from publishers and friends, one in particular identified only as "A," who sent books to her from the Atlanta public library. Her own identification as Southerner, as Catholic, and as writer is strong in her correspondence and one is able to see the entwining of these three aspects of her personality. She commented frequently on the differences she saw between the Catholic and the Protestant world views. She stressed the importance of the Incarnation in her work, and she wrote about what it means to the writer also to be a Christian.

Above all, O'Connor's letters reveal a strong, committed artist, Christian, daughter, and friend. She answered the most difficult questions posed to her by friends who did not understand her Catholicism. She shared with fellow Catholics and non-Catholics

Flannery O'Connor

alike her love for her Church and her Lord. She corrected her correspondents—sometimes quite firmly—when she felt they were wrong, and she often apologized later for her bluntness. But she also encouraged them, sustained them, and nourished them with her wit and insight.

Women's journal writing has become a genre of its own in the twentieth century, but I cannot imagine that O'Connor speaking to herself in diary form could give a reader any more insight into her character than O'Connor in dialogue, which is, essentially, what these letters present.

Born in Savannah, Georgia on March 25, 1925, O'Connor moved to Milledgeville with her mother and seriously ill father when she was twelve. Later, after her father's death, she attended Milledgeville's Georgia State College for Women where she contributed to the college newspaper not as a writer, but as a cartoonist, displaying both an early orientation in the visual arts and a strong sense of irony. These cartoons, highly stylized, often feature a female figure, obviously a caricatured self-portrait, amusingly self-deprecating, offering comments on the social, political, and academic life of a mid-1940's college campus.

Like so many writers early in their careers, O'Connor felt she had to leave home to gain a broader perspective than the one afforded her by rural Georgia life. What she was to discover was that for the artist the entire universe exists in the gesture of the individual, and the individual she knew best was Southern. After she finished her studies in Iowa, she moved to Yaddo, a retreat for writers in New York, spent a few months in New York City and after returning home for a while, moved in September of 1949 into the Connecticut home of Robert and Sally Fitzgerald. When O'Connor became ill late in 1950, she returned to Milledgeville and gradually began to realize that Georgia was where she belonged. For the rest of her life she remained close to home with only occasional forays north for speaking engagements and visits. Due to a deteriorating hip joint, she was on crutches for many of these years and travel was an ordeal for her.

She and her mother did, however, manage a pilgrimage to Rome and Lourdes where, as Flannery reported, Sally Fitzgerald persuaded her to take the healing baths. She wrote in her only letter from Rome: "Lourdes was not as bad as I expected. I took the bath. For a selection of bad motives, such as to prevent any bad conscience for not having done it, and because it seemed at the time that it must be what was wanted of me. I went early in the morning. Only about 40 ahead of me so the water looked pretty clean. They pass around the water for 'les malades' to drink & everybody drinks out of the same cup. As somebody said, the miracle is that the place don't bring on epidemics. Well, I did it all and with very bad grace."[6] Flannery was highly skeptical and definitely reluctant to participate in something she considered unnecessary and maybe even unhealthy. Much to her chagrin and the delight of her elderly cousin who had financed the trip, O'Connor's hip improved a few months later. But she was determined not to undertake such a trip again. For most of the trip's seventeen days she suffered from a virulent cold and later wrote, "We went to Europe and I lived through it but my capacity for staying at home has been perfected, sealed & is going to last me the rest of my life."[7]

Life back in Georgia fell into a routine of morning writing, afternoon reading and talking with occasional visitors, and constant attention to her chickens, peacocks, swans, and Muscovy ducks. The peacocks in particular gave her immense pleasure and she even achieved notoriety as a successful breeder of superior peafowl.

The chief animal keeper at the farm, however, was Regina, her mother. Her influence on her daughter is inestimable, but it is certain that both the "colloquial" and the "Christian" in Flannery's character were gifts from Regina O'Connor. The letters are filled with anecdotes about Regina, whom Flannery affectionately calls "my parent." To Cecil Dawkins, a gifted young writer and regular correspondent, O'Connor wrote in 1959: "The current ordeal is that my mother is now in the process of reading [*The Violent Bear It Away*]. She reads about two pages, gets up and goes to the back door for a conference with Shot, comes back, reads two more pages, gets up and goes to the barn. Yesterday she read a whole chapter. There are twelve chapters. All the time she is reading, I know she would like to be in the yard digging. I think the reason I am a short-story writer is so my mother can read my work in one sitting."[8]

Regina was obviously a strong woman. She had been forced into independence with the death of her husband, and Flannery presented her in the letters as a self-sufficient woman, perfectly capable of caring for a sick daughter, raising a herd of cattle, and handling both the Negroes, who were permanent workers, and the transient farm help. Christmas 1958 brought a description of Regina's firmness and quick wit, traits Flannery herself inherited. She wrote of the farm workers: "Big doings here the other night in preparation for the Yuletide. Louise came over after supper and said she was afraid to go back home because Jack had the gun loaded and said he was going to kill her. He was eventually persuaded by my mother to bring the gun over and leave it in the back hall. After the liquor wore off them, they all calmed down and yesterday she gave him back his gun; but today, we had to stay home to make sure hostilities didn't redevelop. So far nothing. My mother gave them a snappy sermon on: " 'Thou shalt not kill during the Christmas season' when she gave them their presents last night and I guess it paid off . . . ."[9]

Later, after Regina had decided to raise beef rather than dairy cattle, O'Connor related another typical incident: "Everything is in fine shape here since we are no longer in the dairy bidnis. Shot is still incapacitated so we get along with Jack and Louise, but Jack took off last week and stayed all week. He came back this morning, having been beat up in the Negro juke joint. Regina

asked him where he had been and he said he had been plowing
for a crippled man and he went because he knew the Lord would
bless her for doing without him for the week. She said the Lord
would have blessed me just the same if you had told me you
were going."[10] It was not necessary for O'Connor to go even
beyond her back door to find material for her fiction.

In O'Connor's characters and running throughout her own
letters is a streak of humor which is indigenous to the southern
cracker. A combination of mild self-deprecation, irony, vivid
phrasing, and flawless timing, it is the humor that initially turns
a reader's head. She says to one of her correspondents, "I certainly am glad you like the stories because now I feel it's not bad
that I like them so much. The truth is I like them better than
anybody and I read them over and laugh and laugh, then get
embarrassed when I remember I was the one wrote them."[11]

As in her stories, the one-liners in her letters hit the mark.
She writes, "Scratch an Episcopalian and you're liable to find
most anything,"[12] or "I had to read [Wise Blood] over after it came
from the typist's and that was like spending the day eating a
horse blanket."[13]

Toward the end of her life, O'Connor asked a friend to try to
find a picture of a statue she had seen of the Madonna and Child
laughing—not merely smiling, but laughing heartily. Humor was
for O'Connor a necessary ingredient, so her attraction to the
laughing babe who was also to be the suffering Christ was appropriate. For her and for all Christians sorrow and triumph may
be contained in the same image.

It was not her propensity to laughter, however, that provoked
so many young writers to ask O'Connor for advice—both specific
advice about individual stories and more general recommenda-
tions about the writing process itself. She wrote to these literary
newcomers with great seriousness. To Cecil Dawkins, who was
experiencing a dry spell, she wrote: "You ought to set aside three
hours every morning in which you write or do nothing else; no

reading, no talking, no cooking, no nothing, but you sit there. If you write all right and if you don't all right, but you do not read; whether you start something different every day and finish nothing makes no difference; you sit there. It's the only way, I'm telling you. If inspiration comes you are there to receive it, you are not reading."[14]

O'Connor's regimen was to sit at her manual typewriter for two or three hours and follow her characters around. (She said that because the typewriter required more fingers than the pen, it was the more intimate instrument.) She often discarded what she created, but she insisted that what she threw away was valuable because without it she would never have arrived at the good writing. Her pace produced about two pages a day.[15] She did not write from an outline, insisting that her characters could carry the stories by themselves. "Remember," she wrote to her friend, "that you don't write a story because you have an idea but because you have a believable character."[16] She also advised writers to forget about plot when beginning a novel or story. "When you have a character he will create his own situation and his situation will suggest some kind of resolution as you get into it. Wouldn't it be better for you to discover a meaning in what you write than to impose one? Nothing you write will lack meaning because the meaning is in you."[17]

As for technical considerations, such as point of view, O'Connor said she usually didn't think much about it when writing a short story, "but on the novel it gets to be a considerable worry . . . . I seem to stay in a snarl. . . ."[18] She admitted that she had difficulties with omniscient narrators, who must "NEVER speak colloquially."[19]

She was concerned with factual accuracy and when she discovered in the stories of other writers details that were not true to life, she corrected the authors. Cecil Dawkins, for example, placed her black characters in the Georgia mountains. O'Connor wrote her: "Negroes just don't go live in the mountains. At least

there are no Negroes in the Georgia or North Carolina mountains . . . . The sun doesn't set on a Negro in a mountain county.
The people run them out."[20] O'Connor said to another friend
that "the gist and moral of all these unlucid remarks is that all
writing is painful and that if it is not painful then it is not worth
doing."[21]

The connection between her writing and her faith was profound. O'Connor spoke of "self-abandonment," a lack of self-
consciousness which she experienced when she was writing.
She compared this with "Christian self-abandonment,"[22]
suggesting that both in her faith life and in her artistic life, the
self became a vehicle for the Other.[23] God used her and her
talents as an instrument. When this occurred, she was so entirely
immersed in the creative process that she forgot completely about
her own physical situation. Only then could she become a chan-
nel for God's grace and the Holy Spirit's breath.

As a Catholic, O'Connor possessed a sacramental understanding which was to give her art its solid base. She wrote to a
professor, "You said something about my stories dipping into
life—as if this were commendable but a trifle unusual; from
which I get the notion that you may dip largely into your head.
This would be in line with the Protestant temper—approaching
the spiritual directly instead of through matter."[24] Because
O'Connor accepted sacrament as truth, she found it easy to view
the natural things of this world as vehicles or instruments for
God's grace. The concrete, the hearable, sayable, seeable object
or event always possessed sacramental potential. In her stories
the world of matter always exists in order to be used as an entry
to one of God's mysteries, making it acessible, if not completely
understood.

By today's standards, O'Connor was in many of her beliefs a
conservative Catholic, accepting without question, for example,
the Pope's dictum on birth control, writing tersely, "Either practice restraint or be prepared for crowding."[25] She requested offi-

cial permission to read occasional forbidden books on the Catholic Index, and probably would not have read them if she had not received permission. Though she was not comfortable with the spoken English mass, she was, as might be expected, a lover of the liturgy. "So many prayer books are so awful," she wrote in 1956, "but if you stick with the liturgy, you are safe."[26] Liturgy was for O'Connor the careful arrangement of worship so that human weariness, or inattentiveness, or laziness did not intrude upon the worship of an entire congregation. A priest's feelings on a particular day did not change the liturgy. It was consistent and operative, effective in spite of human weakness.

Living in a region fraught with tritely emotional religious expression, Flannery O'Connor distrusted feelings as an indicator of faith. She wrote at length about this and other Christian issues to "A." "There is a question whether faith can or is supposed to be emotionally satisfying. I must say that the thought of everyone lolling about in an emotionally satisfying faith is repugnant to me. I believe that we are ultimately directed Godward but that this journey is often impeded by emotion."[27] As she wrote later, "We [Catholics] don't believe grace is something you have to feel. The Catholic always distrusts his emotional reaction to the sacraments."[28]

O'Connor was often critical of what she considered Protestant shortcomings. "A Protestant habit," she writes, "is to condemn the Church for being authoritarian and then blame her for not being authoritarian enough."[29] But she had a healthy respect for fundamentalist Protestants. She was alarmed at the liberal theology she heard coming from some Protestant camps and she wrote, "One of the effects of modern liberal Protestantism has been gradually to turn religion into poetry and therapy, to make truth vaguer and vaguer and more and more relative, to banish intellectual distinctions, to depend on feeling instead of thought, and gradually to come to believe that God has no power, that he cannot communicate with us, cannot reveal himself to us, indeed has not done so and that religion is our own sweet invention."[30] She understood the difference between cheap grace and costly grace. "What people don't realize," she wrote to Louise Abbot, "is how much religion costs. They think faith is a big electric blanket, when of course it is the cross."[31] O'Connor felt the fundamentalist Protestant churches were closer to Rome than they realized, even though many still considered the Catholic church the arch-enemy. The grand equalizer was the universal experience of existential unbelief, which O'Connor considered to be the necessary starting point of faith. She reminded one correspondent of a plea she attributed to Peter (actually the words were spoken by the father of an epileptic boy—Mark 9:24): "Lord, I believe. Help my unbelief."[32] She pointed out to Cecil Dawkins that the founder of the Church was the same man "who denied Christ three times and couldn't walk on the water by himself."[33]

O'Connor was realistic about human nature and its ability to resist grace.[34] She understood the ebbs and flows of faith peculiar to humankind. Perhaps because she felt that conversion was a continuing process,[35] she was troubled but not burdened when her friends experienced momentary setbacks in their faith lives. She wrote to "A" who had converted to Catholicism and was now filled with doubts, "Some people when they lose their faith in Christ, substitute a swollen faith in themselves. I think you are too honest for that, that you never had much faith in yourself in the first place and that now that you don't believe in Christ, you will believe even less in yourself; which itself is regrettable, but let me tell you this: faith comes and goes."[36]

O'Connor's conviction that our age is deaf and blind to truth appears in all of her writings. How to gain the attention of a handicapped generation is her constant concern. She does it by exaggeration, shouting, or drawing very large pictures, and recommends pushing "as hard as the age that pushes against you."[37]

Perhaps the violence that shocks so many first-time readers of O'Connor's fiction seems so unpalatable because it is so personal.

We encounter violence daily, but most often at a distance. O'Connor counteracts the desensitizing effect of remote violence by forcing it upon us in a form we cannot escape. Whether it is the drowning of a child in a river, or the murder of an old man in the stairwell of his apartment building, or the massacre of an entire family on a deserted Georgia road, O'Connor pushes her readers to the brink over and over again. "The kingdom of heaven," she writes, "has to be taken by violence or not at all."[38] These stories are particularly difficult for the secular "good man," who will not find in them many examples of the godly life, but who will be continually challenged to define and redefine his own conception of goodness. She wrote to Cecil Dawkins, "It's not a matter in these stories of Do Unto Others. That can be found in any ethical culture series. It is the fact of the Word made flesh."[39] She goes on to identify this emphasis as not only Roman Catholic, but as orthodox Protestant belief, too.

O'Connor always pushes us back to the agonizing scandal of the cross. That scandal has at its heart the recognition that humanity is fallen and needs redemption. Perhaps because the South still smarts from its own fall in the War Between the States, redemption has a special meaning. (Confederate Memorial Day is still a state holiday in Georgia.) With defeat comes the realization that humanity alone cannot save itself, humanity alone cannot perfect itself, humanity alone is vulnerable and weak. In 1958 O'Connor wrote to Cecil Dawkins saying that "the Liberal approach is that man has never fallen, never incurred guilt, and is ultimately perfectable by his own efforts. Therefore, evil in this light is a problem of better housing, sanitation, health, etc. and all the mysteries will eventually be cleared up."[40]

Of course, for the Christian the mysteries remain mysterious to the end. Perhaps this recognition that not all human motivation and behavior can be explained completely accounts for O'Connor's strong feelings against the social sciences (ironic because she was a social-science major in college). In her letters she frequently deplored the social scientist's propensity for de-humanizing lingo. In particular, the Freudians irritated her. In one letter she berated William Sessions for his Freudian interpretations: "I do hope . . . that you will get over the kind of thinking that sees in every door handle a phallic symbol . . . . The Freudian technique can be applied to anything at all with equally ridiculous results. My Lord, Billy, recover your simplicity. You ain't in Manhattan. Don't inflict that stuff on the poor students there; they deserve better."[41]

In many letters O'Connor referred in a disapproving tone to academics in general and English teachers in particular. At Wesleyan she had read "A Good Man Is Hard to Find" and after the reading entertained questions. One teacher asked why The Misfit's hat was black and what it meant. She answered that country men wore black hats and they did it to cover their heads.[42] Another letter to an English professor deserves quoting in its entirety. The professor also had questions about "A Good Man . . . ," explaining that three professors and ninety students had come to the following conclusions: "Bailey, we believe, imagines the appearance of the Misfit . . . . Bailey, we further believe, identifies himself with the Misfit and so plays two roles in the imaginary last half of the story. But we cannot, after great effort, determine the point at which reality fades into illusion or reverie. Does the accident literally occur, or is it a part of Bailey's dream?"[43] O'Connor replied:

The interpretation of your ninety students and three teachers is fantastic and about as far from my intentions as it could get to be. If it were a legitimate interpretation, the story would be little more than a trick and its interest would be simply for abnormal psychology. I am not interested in abnormal psychology.

. . . Bailey's only importance is as the Grandmother's boy and the driver of the car. It is the Grandmother who first recognizes the Misfit and who is most concerned with him throughout. The story is a duel of sorts between the Grandmother and her superficial beliefs and the Misfit's more profoundly felt involvement with Christ's action which set the world off balance for him.

The meaning of a story should go on expanding for the reader the more he thinks about it, but meaning cannot be captured in an interpretation. If teachers are in the habit of approaching a story as if it were a research problem for which any answer is believable as long as it is not obvious, then I think students will never learn to enjoy fiction. Too much interpretation is certainly worse than too little, and where feeling for a story is absent, theory will not supply it.

My tone is not meant to be obnoxious. I am in a state of shock.[44]

One of O'Connor's final letters was to another professor of English and referred to her story, "Greenleaf": "Thank you for your note. I'm sorry I can't answer it more fully but I am in the hospital and not up to literary questions . . . . As for Mrs. May, I must have named her that because I knew some English teacher would write and ask me why. I think you folks sometime strain the soup too thin."[45] In another letter she threw up her hands and said of a well-known literary critic, "Can it be possible that a man with this much learning knows so little about Christianity?"[46] That was the problem she faced every time she published anything. She was writing for an audience for whom the Incarnation had little meaning, and yet her fiction over and over again showed common people encountering the terror, mystery, and beauty of the Word made flesh. She might have predicted that many of her readers would be mildly puzzled, if not completely confounded.

Reading through the letters, one cannot help but notice certain similarities between O'Connor's life and the lives of her characters. In the early letters, she and her mother were preparing for a refugee family, similar to the Guizacs in "The Displaced Person." She also wrote that "the two colored people in 'The Displaced Person' are on this place now. The old man is 84 but vertical or more or less so. He doesn't see too good and the other day he fertilized some of my mother's bulbs with worm medicine for the calves."[47]

Life was a strange imitation of fiction when Flannery, her mother, and Catharine Carver visited the Cyclorama in Atlanta where Enoch in *Wise Blood* stole the mummy: "Catharine wanted to see the mummy herself, so she and Regina went upstairs to look for it and I waited downstairs. After a while they came back but hadn't found it. On the way out, Catharine asked the girl at the ticket place if there had used to be one and the girl said yes there had, but she didn't know what had happened to it. Catharine was satisfied that Enoch had taken it."[48]

That fiction contained truth was the conviction that Flannery O'Connor lived with every day. That this truth was sometimes odd or uncomfortable or violent, that it was often pictured and realized in the grotesque, O'Connor faced unflinchingly. Quoting Robert Fitzgerald, O'Connor wrote, "It is the business of the artist to uncover the strangeness of truth."[49] What could be stranger than a God who decides to suffer with us? What could be more uncomfortable or more violent than the cross? What could be more comically grotesque than an individual trying to escape his own identity as God's child and in his rush out the temple door, smacking straight into the Incarnation?

Flannery O'Connor's meaning is in her stories because it was in her life. She knew that one can never "put meaning in." It is implicit in the characters in a work of fiction as much as in an individual's personal existence.

Toward the end of O'Connor's letters, one experiences a depressing sense of inevitability. As one approaches August 3, 1964, the temptation is simply to stop reading—as if that would somehow suspend the ending. Her final letter, written on July 29th, 1964, was found on her nightstand after her death. Sally Fitzgerald notes that it is almost illegible. It is playful in its nicknaming, but serious in its brief contents, which refer to an anonymous phone call her friend received. "Be properly scared," O'Connor advises, "and go on doing what you have to do, but take the necessary precautions . . . . Cheers, Tarfunk."[50]

Such proper scaring is what many of O'Connor's characters and all of her readers require and experience in her fiction. We must go on doing what we have to do, but with clearer eyes and more sensitive ears, having run into Truth along the way.

— 2 —

The Law
Which Condemns

First responses to O'Connor are invariably extreme. Forgetting about the stoning of St. Stephen or Herod's slaughter of the innocents or even the cross itself, many first-time readers of O'Connor, knowing only that she is a Christian writer, are puzzled by her grotesqueries and the violence of her vision. The problem is, of course, that most readers possess flimsy ideas about what is "Christian" literature and what is not. In a review written in 1956 O'Connor claimed that "virtue can believably triumph only in completely drawn characters and against a background whose roots are recognized to be in original sin."[1] The characters in O'Connor's stories find grace, but between their flight from the City of Destruction and their arrival at the gates of the Heavenly City, they must encounter the trauma of the cross.

No matter how you read it, the gospel contains birth in a cold, dirty stable and violent death on Golgotha. The Incarnation finds its actual fulfillment in the Resurrection, but resurrection can occur only after death. O'Connor understood that this is one hard fact humankind would rather ignore, and her characters show extraordinary initiative and ingenuity in finding ways to avoid confronting their frailties, the chief of which is their own mortality. It is often only when a character smacks flat up against death that the necessity of salvation is finally apparent. That is why so many of O'Connor's stories reach a violent climax, forcing the characters to see grace in a new and terrible way.

Sight and insight are intimately connected metaphors in O'Connor's stories—for both character and reader. Josephine Hendin has adopted the phrase "comic literalization" to describe the metaphorical development in these works. "Beginning with a metaphoric statement," she writes, "the story develops as the metaphor becomes realized in a concrete action or material object."[2] At key moments—often at the height of a story's crisis, sometimes at a moment of foreshadowing—O'Connor clicks the camera and catches a strange picture. In the seventeenth century, these would have been called *emblems;* the fictive moment containing them, the emblematic moment.

As early as 1943-45 O'Connor had displayed an interest and talent for this sort of exaggerated visual representation in the cartoons she drew for the weekly student newspaper at Georgia State College for Women. Although these cartoons are not emblems, they do demonstrate both her preoccupation with capturing a representative moment in pictorial form and a rare facility for creating caricature for the purpose of social and political commentary. In her stories she adds a further dimension to these moments, transforming them into spiritual epiphanies.

For the seventeenth-century reader emblems were the pictorial representations of scriptural truth—highly exaggerated yet literal. Thus, the picture used in Francis Quarles's emblem book, *Emblems, Divine and Moral* (1635) to illustrate the verse, "Stay my steps in thy paths that my feet do not slide" (Psalm 17:5) shows a person in a child's walker being led through the streets by an angelic creature. The steps are literally "stayed." The feet do not slide because the walker supports and the angel guides. Emblems literalized a motto, epigram, or scriptural passage to provoke a new response to an old and often too familiar saying.

O'Connor's emblems work in similar ways. She often paints

"Business as Usual"

Cartoon originally published in "Colonnade," volume XVII, no. 12, p. 4, January 2, 1943, Georgia College, Milledgeville, Georgia.

stark pictures which draw attention to themselves both picto-
rially, as still moments caught in time, and emblematically, as
exaggerated representations of deeper spiritual truths. In "The
Geranium" the flower pot crashes to the pavement, and the
flowers lie on the ground, roots in the air. The camera clicks. In
"The Barber" Rayber runs out of the barber shop, his bib still
on, lather dripping from his chin. The camera clicks again. In
"Revelation" Mrs. Turpin, leaning on the fence, turns the water
on the hogs. In "Parker's Back" Parker leaves his shoes burning
in the middle of the field. In each of O'Connor's stories, the
climactic moment could be lifted from a seventeenth-century
emblem book. These moments are often violent, bizarre, surprising. The Christ tattooed on Parker's back is beaten with a broom.
The old lady whose family has just been shot reaches in sudden
affection for her killer. The child drowns in the river in which
he has been baptized.

Peter Daly points out that emblematic thinking, with all of its
shocking grotesqueries, proves most puzzling to the twentieth-
century reader, whose sensibilities do not accord with those of
the sixteenth or seventeenth-century emblem-book reader. His
description of the "emblematic world view" is, however, relevant
to this study of O'Connor's fiction:

> The emblematic world view is . . . based on the emblematic
> mode of thought, which sees inherent meaning in the objects
> of nature and human history. The attitude of Bunyan, Grim-
> melshausen, and Defoe . . . is fundamentally emblematic in
> that they regard the world and nature as "a giant canvas upon
> which God has stroken in a wealth of moral meaning."[3]

O'Connor did not, so far as we can determine, use the emblem-
books as sources. There is no direct evidence that she was con-
versant with the tradition, but I take my cue from Peter Daly
who suggests that there is a respectable body of literary criticism

which has "interpreted literature against the general background of emblem-books, using them not as sources but as parallels, or keys, to the understanding of literature."[4] Another major thinker in the field of emblem literature is Rosemary Freeman, who has pointed out that emblem-books flourished at a time when allegory was also popular, that in fact "the taste for emblems was part of a wider taste for allegory."[5] There is little room in twentieth-century literature for allegory, perhaps because it suggests a cosmos of absolute moral values, and this is not a currently popular perception. But O'Connor, whose universe was imbued with these absolute moral values, was never bothered by intellectual fads. In her personal copy of William James's *The Varieties of Religious Experience: A Study in Human Nature*, O'Connor marked the following passage:

> In the Louvre there is a picture, by Guido Reni, of St. Michael with his foot on Satan's neck. The richness of the picture is in large part due to the fiend's figure being there. The richness of its allegorical meaning also is due to his being there—that is, the world is all the richer for having a devil in it, so long as we keep our foot upon his neck. In the religious consciousness, that is just the position in which the fiend, the negative or tragic principle, is found.[6]

That O'Connor understood the ways in which allegory could be used to enrich the fictive vision is evident from her admiration for Hawthorne, even though she claimed to rely on allegory less than he did. One critic has suggested that for O'Connor allegory was a "way of seeing the concrete situation most fully."[7] She was familiar with the medieval, fourfold method of interpreting Scripture (literal, allegorical, tropological and anagogical),[8] and her readings indicate that she was exposed to authors who understood the fullness of allegory. Ulanov, for example, describes the literature of allegory as being "predicated upon clear convictions about the natural order." He observes that this type of literature "moves quite normally from this world to the next" and that "in that movement, nothing known to man need be by-passed. Every discipline, every experience can be productive of revelations. The chaff, when husked, always reveals the wheat."[9] He further insists that "the allegorical method is not easily understood if one treats it mechanically." In a personal copy of *The Sewanee Review* O'Connor's marginalia indicate her feelings about the modern reader's ability to understand Christian allegory. The article she read was J. A. Bryant's "Shakespeare's Allegory: *The Winter's Tale*," in which the author contended that Shakespeare may have shaped the play's theme of Christian grace by "drawing unconsciously upon a doctrinal pattern so inextricably woven into the contemporary fabric of belief that even the barest hint of it in the material he was working on could make it operative." O'Connor has marked this passage and written next to it: "how much dogma left operative now?"[10]

How to capture the attention of a world in which traditional scriptural truths no longer had meaning—this was O'Connor's challenge. Her writing, grounded in this concrete and fallen world, has been called the fiction of the grotesque. The word is descriptive of her characters who are often unlovable, caricatured, and deliberately distorted. O'Connor is, of course, showing us ourselves. We cannot dismiss any of her characters as unworthy of grace without dismissing ourselves, too. Sin has done its job with even the most righteous. Usually the most self-righteous and moral of O'Connor's characters turn out to be the blindest, needing God most desperately and often capable of recognizing Him only in the oddest, most distorted forms. Again, these characters are ourselves, the readers of O'Connor's fiction—and to read O'Connor is to enter a world laden with religious artifacts which require our response.

Although Maureen Quilligan does not consider O'Connor in *The Language of Allegory*, her words provide the appropriate directive for O'Connor's readers: "Once we get past the necessary complexities of the text and have a measure of control over our response to it, we will be able to see that the proper reader of allegory . . . [is] someone who is willing to entertain the possibility of making a religious reponse to the ineffability invoked by its polysemous language."[11] Thomas Linehan puts it more simply: "In story after story, Flannery O'Connor expands upon a religious theme which can be described in brief terms. To her readers she says, 'Come to your senses!'"[12]

O'Connor's early work contains hints of what was to develop more fully later. In "The Geranium," "The Barber," "The Crop," and "The Turkey," all written before 1949, one finds the grotesque, the violent, and the alienated. One is aware of the oddly pictorial, and also the presence of the law, which grace continually tries to supplant.

Her first publication, "The Geranium," is the story of distances and isolation. Old Dudley has been displaced; from a small Southern town he moves to New York City to live with his daughter. She has introduced him to the depths of the subway, the heights of the El, the "halls that reminded [him] of tape measures strung out with a door every inch,"[13] the stairs which he climbs and descends to identical floors and identical apartments. He often gets lost.

His universe eventually contracts to the size of one small apartment. Old Dudley's world has changed, most disappointingly. Nature for him must now fit into the geranium pot placed on the window ledge of the apartment across the back alley. This geranium reminds him both of the drapes back home and of the Grisby boy, "who had polio and had to be wheeled out every morning and left in the sun to blink."[14] The bow decorating the pot recalls for him the bow on the Sunday uniform of the black woman who cooked for his boarding house.

The window he looks out of in New York looks only on other windows, so different from the window at home which looked out on the river. A prisoner, he can only watch and be watched through panes of glass. Old Dudley has, however, freely chosen this prison and he realizes that it is his own fault; he should not have given in to curiosity about the big city. He should never have consented to leave his home.

Perhaps because he has exercised free will and made the wrong choice, Dudley now feels particularly tied to a stolid orderliness. He has been excluded from Paradise and now his life is ordered by the law. When the geranium does not appear at precisely 10:15, he becomes anxious. Like the law which both orders and condemns, the world of routine and orderliness has become both his closest ally (the one thing he can depend on) and in the form of the neighborhood's bland sameness, his greatest enemy. He gets lost, he has discovered, in the uniformity of the buildings surrounding him, and even in his own building.

Finally, we see that he is fatally tied not only to physical orderliness, but also to his old sense of propriety. His idea of social order is violated by the black man who moves in next door, who calls him "old-timer" and guides him back to his door, his hand on his arm. Shattered by this experience, Dudley sits in the chair by the window, crying.

Old Dudley wants more than what he has been given. He wants to retreat to his past and all he finds most comfortable there, not recognizing the contradictory nature of his behavior. He does not want change within the confines of his present life. He needs predictability. And yet, of course, what he wants most desperately is change.

His daughter is laboring under a similar sense of the law—for her, the concept of "duty": "She was seeing that her father spent his last years with his own family and not in a decayed boarding house full of old women whose heads jiggled. She was doing her duty. She had brothers and sisters who were not."[15]

"The Geranium" is a story of handicaps—Old Dudley's, the daughter's, nature's itself—all fallen and all somewhat pre-gospel. The final "fall" of the geranium pot to the ground below provokes Old Dudley's resolve to retrieve the geranium himself, but then he realizes that he must travel through a hellish landscape to get there:

> He'd go down and pick it up. He'd put it in his own window and look at it all day if he wanted to. He turned from the window and left the room. He walked slowly down the dog run and got to the steps. The steps dropped down like a deep wound in the floor. They opened up through a gap like a cavern and went down and down. And he had gone up them a little behind the nigger. And the nigger had pulled him up on his feet and kept his arm in his and gone up the steps with him and said he hunted deer, "old-timer," and seen him holding a gun that wasn't there and sitting on the steps like a child. He had shiny tan shoes and he was trying not to laugh and the whole business was laughing. There'd probably be niggers with black flecks in their socks on every step, pulling down their mouths so as not to laugh. The steps dropped down and down. He wouldn't go down and have niggers pattin' him on the back. He went back to the room and the window and looked down at the geranium.[16]

Dudley chooses a narrower hell. He decides not to upset his own social mores, not to risk an encounter with the black man on his way down, not to retrieve the geranium—the only part of his present life which provides a link with his past. He is locked in a tortuous limbo, uprooted like the geranium, but unwilling and unable to find new soil. In a way, he is modern humanity itself. The camera clicks in this story to show Dudley framed by the window from which he looks into the frame of another window across the alley. His environment contains its own still shots and its own picture frame. The final photograph is of that geranium, which has fallen out of the picture and therefore, out of Dudley's reach.

O'Connor does not deal overtly with the gospel in this story, as she does in so many of her later stories, but she does use a displaced person as her major character and she also shows how legalism reinforces loneliness. The displaced person will appear in her writing, culminating in the story by that name. The legalistic, lonely individual will be her major female character in many of her stories of rural farm life.

Two of her early stories, "The Barber" and "The Crop," deal with Walter Mitty-type characters who, unlike old Dudley, live in community, though even within that community they are alienated individuals. "The Barber" finds Rayber the odd man out. He is not an intellectual and he is not a barber, but he attempts to construct a political argument which would convince both his philosopher friend and his barber that he is not a fool for supporting the liberal candidate. The story is really about blindness. Rayber believes he sees clearly, but his position paper ends with this pronouncement: "Men who use ideas without measuring them are walking on wind."[17] In castigating others, he unwittingly castigates himself, for he certainly does not "measure" his ideas. He finally articulates his political position not verbally, not rationally, but physically, violently. He slugs the barber and runs out of the shop still bibbed and half-lathered.

In "The Crop" O'Connor presents an even more obvious Mitty. This is O'Connor's only story about a writer, a character trapped in a "system" of household orderliness. Her morning task is to crumb the table, and as she does so, the reader glimpses the emblem of an entire culture dwindling into routine and old age. But unlike Old Dudley, Willie does not allow the system to intrude upon her imaginative life.

Willie possesses at least one of Flannery's own writing habits: she sits at her typewriter from morning to noon, but unlike O'Connor, Willie never writes much. "There were so many subjects to write stories about that Miss Willerton never could think of one."[18] She looks for stories with "social tension," discarding bakers and teachers as suitable candidates for characters because "they weren't even a social problem."[19] She finally decides to write about a sharecropper, despite the fact that she has never met one. What follows is her own fantasy as she dreams herself into the plot, and is finally interrupted by Miss Lucia who asks her to run some errands. Her story never progresses beyond the third sentence because when she returns, she decides instead to write about the Irish.

One is reminded of O'Connor's comments at a writer's conference, after reading several of the participants' manuscripts. "After this experience," she said, "I found myself ready to admit, if not that the short story is one of the most difficult literary forms, at least that it is more difficult for some than for others. I still suspect that most people start out with some kind of ability to tell a story but that it gets lost along the way." Later she was to say, "The more stories I write, the more mysterious I find the process and the less I find myself capable of analyzing it."[20]

"The Turkey," another of O'Connor's early stories, introduces the mystery of God's grace which permeates her later fiction. This is the first story, excluding portions of her early novel *Wise Blood*, that deals overtly with the matter of law and grace. In this story one sees no easy answers about God. Ruller, age 11, spends most of the first few pages chasing a wounded turkey. Finally, he literally chases it to death, claims it, and returns to town with it proudly slung over his shoulder. The story is, in many ways, a version of the classic initiation story, in which a hero comes of age and proves himself by undergoing a series of trials or tests. Often, as in Faulkner's "The Bear," this test involves the stalking, hunting and killing of a wild animal. Could it be possible that Flannery was parodying Faulkner in entitling *her* initiation story not "The Bear," but "The Turkey"?[21] What makes "The Turkey" more than just standard fare, however, is first of all, Ruller's ultimate loss of the turkey, and second (and more important) the genesis and development in Ruller of a spiritual sensibility.

Near the beginning of the story, after the chase has been under way for some time, Ruller, like Parker in "Parker's Back," runs into a tree and is knocked breathless. "It was like someone had played a dirty trick on him,"[22] he thought. But like Parker it is this violent setback which becomes the first step toward revelation. It should come as no surprise to the reader that a tree, long a symbol of the cross, is here the agent of revelation. It is not so much that Ruller is chasing the turkey, but that God is chasing Ruller, and here again the emblematic camera catches the action at the instant grace intrudes. Ruller lies on the ground for a few minutes, trying to catch his breath. Then he begins to think. "Nuts," he says first. Then he thinks, "Oh hell."

> "Oh hell," he said cautiously.
> Then in a minute he said just, "Hell."
> Then he said it like Hane said it, pulling the e-ull out and trying to get the look in his eye that Hane got. Once Hane said, "God!" and his mother stomped after him and said, "I don't want to hear you say that again. Thou shalt not take the name of the Lord, Thy God, in vain. Do you hear me?" and he guessed that shut Hane up. Ha! He guessed she dressed him off that time.
> "God," he said.
> He looked studiedly at the ground, making circles in the dust with his finger. "God!" he repeated.[23]

Pronouncing *hell* leads Ruller almost immediately to pronouncing *God*. Profanity, which is verbal disrespect for something sacred, depends on the existence of the sacred for its effect. Without the sacred, profanity would merely be words without shock impact. For O'Connor and all Christians, hell is connected with judgment, eternal loss, and separation from God, but to be separated from God, the possibility of union with Him must first exist. In any philosophical system that does not include God, hell of course is meaningless. So, quite naturally, hell leads Ruller to at least pronounce God's name, if not actually ponder Him. Here, as with so many of O'Connor's characters the profane moment becomes the entry point for God's grace—and it is also a moment of tremendous visual interest for the reader. Notice that Ruller accompanies his pronouncement of God's name with a significant gesture. He draws circles in the dusty ground, just as Jesus drew in the dirt when confronted with the Pharisees' questions. Almost immediately, however, Ruller turns the name of the Lord into a deeper profanity:

> "God dammit," he said softly. He could feel his face getting hot and his chest thumping all of a sudden inside. "God dammit to hell," he said almost inaudibly. He looked over his shoulder but no one was there.
> "God dammit to hell, good Lord from Jerusalem," he said. His uncle said "Good Lord from Jerusalem."
> "Good Father, good God, sweep the chickens out the yard," he said and began to giggle. His face was very red . . . . "Our Father who art in heaven, shoot 'em six and roll 'em seven," he said, giggling again.[24]

Again, Ruller cannot sustain his blasphemy. It leads him into an unwitting, silly, irreverent prayer, but it *is* prayer, a request that God will "sweep the chickens out the yard." Soon he will catch the turkey.

He is conscious, throughout, of another presence—a presence which makes his face red and hot, an involuntary sign of guilt. He feels judged and convicted and his human response is to redden, to laugh nervously, and then to counter it all with a bit of bravado: "He might as well go home. What did he want to be sitting around here for? He felt suddenly like he would if people had been laughing at him. Aw, go to hell, he told them. He got up and kicked his foot sharply into somebody's leg and said, 'Take that, sucker . . . .' "[25]

A change is beginning to take place in Ruller for now he finds himself actually addressing God, as if the Almighty were standing there next to him. He is imagining his return home and the way he would explain his torn clothes. He would say that he fell into a hole and he asks, "What difference would it make? Yeah, God, what difference would it make? He almost stopped. He had never heard himself think that tone before."[26] He is apprehensive and appalled and wonders if he is going bad, like his brother Hane. He is not only talking to God, he is flippantly asking him what difference it would make if he lied. This God to whom he speaks is powerless, he concludes, and somewhat tricky. This God gave him a turkey to chase and then did not allow him to catch it. He looks around, feeling someone's eyes.

The eyes are the turkey's and they are also God's. In fact, for Ruller the turkey becomes God's agent, if not God Himself. Ruller possesses a strong sense of God's intervention to save him from a bad end. "If you want me to take [the turkey], he said, I'll be glad to. Maybe finding the turkey was a sign. Maybe God wanted him to be a preacher . . . . He guessed God had stopped him before it was too late. He should be very thankful. Thank you, he said."[27]

Ruller has stumbled on a truth. The turkey is God's gift to him, but he does not know yet what kind of gift he has been given. He struts through town with his catch slung over his shoulder. Filled with pride at being God's chosen one, he decides he should do something for God. In fact, as the minutes pass, he begins desperately to desire something to do for God. He prays to God to send him a beggar. "He had never thought before of praying on his own, but it was a good idea. God had put the turkey there. He'd send him a beggar. He knew for a fact God would send him one."[28] God does send him one—almost immediately. Ruller thrusts his only dime at her and runs away fast. Like the rich young ruler of Luke 18, Ruller (ruler) has acquired a fatal self-righteousness along with his "good deed." The law has led him to sin, not to salvation. It has measured him and he has fallen short. Within minutes the turkey is snatched from him by some rough country boys. Ruller must learn that no one can do anything *for* God. One can only accept God's gifts, freely given, and pass them humbly on to others. A dime is not enough. Only the whole turkey will do.

Ruller realizes at the end of the story that God cannot be manipulated, that when one asks God for a sign or a favor, God answers, but He means literally what He says and He interprets literally one's prayer requests. When Ruller prays for a beggar, he is given one—but this beggar does not need money. She needs food and attention, the two things Ruller most certainly will not give her. After thrusting his dime at her, he rushes off, a warm glow invading his being, thinking that maybe he would give her every cent he had.

God is inscrutable, he discovers, as he runs home without his turkey "certain that Something Awful was tearing behind him with its arms rigid and its fingers ready to clutch."[29] Ruller now becomes the one chased—and he is just beginning to understand that the God who is chasing him is different from the one he had imagined so impudently before.

Manley Pointer, the Bible salesman in "Good Country People," is an older version of the child running away from God's clutches. An inversion of Hazel Motes in *Wise Blood*, Manley preaches too much, and too loudly. He preaches not the gospel, but the necessity of having a Bible in one's parlor. He is ostensibly attracted to Hulga-Joy because of her open declaration of atheism and when he discovers that she has been attracted to him by his supposedly innocent Christian faith, he grabs her artificial leg and runs, stuffing the leg into his valise with both the true and the false Bibles. One feels his ambivalence—he cannot make up his mind. Drawn inexplicably to the Word, he takes every opportunity to prove to himself that the Word is no word at all, but just a false cover for something else.

"Good Country People" opens with the metaphor of the machine, an image which informs the entire story. Mrs. Freeman, "besides the neutral expression that she wore when she was alone . . . had two others, forward and reverse, that she used for all her human dealings. Her forward expression was steady and driving like the advance of a heavy truck."[30] Intractable and unyielding, often she simply comes to a complete stop. The image is picked up in Joy's artificial leg, another "machine" of locomotion on which she clumps about heavily in order to annoy her mother. When Joy decides to change her name to Hulga, it reminds her mother of "the broad blank hull of a battleship,"[31] another massive transport vehicle. And O'Connor describes Hulga's response to her former name, Joy, as "purely mechanical."

This machine-like response is common to all of the characters in the story. Mrs. Hopewell cannot speak in anything but predictable catch-phrases and clichés. "Nothing is perfect. This was one of Mrs. Hopewell's favorite sayings. Another was: that is life! And still another, the most important, was: well, other people have their opinions too."[32] Her encounter with the Bible salesman releases them all in one trite flood: "Why!" she cried, "good country people are the salt of the earth! Besides, we all have different ways of doing, it takes all kinds to make the world go round. That's life!"[33]

The Bible belongs in the parlor, Manley Pointer tells Mrs. Hopewell, but she insists that it is all a matter of taste, which is precisely what religious expression and practice are for her and for so many of O'Connor's good country people, blinded to the gospel and accustomed to religion as a social form only. Though the law is usually all they see, blind, ignorant children that they are, they do not even take the law seriously.

Hulga-Joy has "the look of someone who has achieved blindness by an act of will and means to keep it."[34] Even though she has a Ph.D. in philosophy, she still behaves like a child, pouting,

"Oh well. I can always be a Ph.D."

Cartoon originally published in "Colonnade," volume XVIII, no. 24, p. 2, April 3, 1943, Georgia College, Milledgeville, Georgia.

sullen to her mother, and sarcastic in all of her responses. She
is thirty-two and dresses in a yellow sweat shirt imprinted with
a cowboy and a horse. She shows no sign of being able to care
for herself, but seems to be arrested emotionally somewhere
between childhood and adulthood, even though she is over-
developed intellectually. Curiously, she perceives her mother's
blindness, but not her own. "Woman!" she screams at her
mother. "Do you ever look inside? Do you ever look inside and
see what you are *not*? God! . . . Malebranche was right: we are
not our own light. We are not our own light!"[35]

In spite of all of her beliefs, or lack of them, she is attracted
to Manley Pointer and plans to seduce him. With such an act
she would, of course, be able to reveal his own hypocrisy to
him, and then take his guilt and "change it into a deeper understanding of life." She believes she sees "through" things to Nothing. "We are all damned," she says to him, "but some of us have
taken off our blindfolds and see that there's nothing to see. It's
a kind of salvation."[36]

Early in the story, Mrs. Hopewell recognizes a bond between
Manley and her daughter in their shared heart "conditions."
Hulga's is a serious heart condition which will, the doctors say,
take her life within a few years. Manley says he, too, has a heart
problem which will soon lead to his death. There is no way of
knowing for sure if he speaks metaphorically or literally. But
even if he does not suffer from physiological heart disease, his
heart *is* the heart of his problem. Both Hulga's and Manley's
hearts are infected with a more profound and deadly disease
than could ever be manifested physically. Hulga has all her life
ignored her heart in favor of her head. In fact, when she is kissed
for the first time, it "produced that extra surge of adrena-
lin . . . that enables one to carry a packed trunk out of a burning
house, but in her, the power went at once to the brain."[37] Later
in the hayloft with Manley "her mind . . . never stopped or lost
itself for a second to her feelings."[38] Only when he asks for the

ultimate intimacy—for her to show him how her artificial leg is attached—does she give in to her heart, realizing both a physical and mysterious attraction to her seducer. The experience is expressed in heavily religious terms. She is moved by the boy's declaration that her leg has made her unlike anyone else.

> She decided that for the first time in her life she was face to face with real innocence. This boy, with an instinct that came from beyond wisdom, had touched the truth about her. When after a minute, she said in a hoarse high voice, "All right," it was like surrendering to him completely. It was like losing her own life and finding it again, miraculously, in his.[39]

Hulga is hungry for an encounter with true innocence. She notices that Manley's "breath was clear and sweet like a child's and the kisses were sticky like a child's."[40] But her preconceptions are shattered when he opens his valise to reveal two Bibles: one true, the other with a false binding which opens to disclose a flask, a deck of lewdly decorated playing cards, and a package of prophylactics. Attracted to her professed atheism, he does not realize what the traditional symbols of sin and vice will do to her, for she has been attracted to *his* professed innocence. She screams for her leg. He is puzzled. "What's the matter with you all of a sudden? . . . You just a while ago said you didn't believe in nothing. I thought you was some girl!"[41]

He takes her leg away—her support, her independence, her privacy, her pride, and he leaves her vulnerable, with her flaws exposed. The leg is thrust into the valise with the true and the false Bibles. And here is the emblem—of the devil running away with a false leg in his valise—except that, of course, Manley is both child and devil at once and this is what so puzzles Hulga at the end of the story. It is the truth with which she must contend, however, for it is the truth of the human predicament. Just as Manley has always carried his two Bibles with him, Hulga has worn her false leg every day next to her true leg. She is a living contradiction, a mix of both real and artificial, just as Manley carries with him both virtue and sin. The point is that the sins (Manley's rather too obvious symbols of gambling, drinking and fornication) are only half of the story for each of the characters. The other half is the gospel, the Word, which exists right next to the sins of the world—in the same briefcase, in fact. For both Hulga and Manley, that becomes the only place the gospel can be apprehended.

When Manley breaks through the barrier of Hulga's intellect, for the very first time in her life she *feels* something. It is vague, it is unsettling, and it turns out to have been based on a mutual misinterpretation, but this does not seem to matter. For O'Connor shows us once again that grace chooses the most profane moment to appear.

In the first paragraph of the story Mrs. Freeman points to the canned figs on the top shelf, collecting dust. Figs have long been associated with fertility in scriptural and other writings. Here they are uneaten; they gather dust, but they are at least still available. Fecundity does not seem to be a possibility for Hulga, who is contrasted early in the story with Mrs. Freeman's pregnant, fifteen-year-old daughter. But the final scene in the hay loft is in certain respects reminiscent of the traditional nativity scene, complete with straw and gentle light, "filled with dust particles," only, of course, the birth is to be Hulga's, and in a sense here she becomes her own child. Even Manley's prophylactics are appropriate to the imagery. They are kept in his false Bible and are designed to inhibit birth or the growth of new life. The true Word, on the other hand, will lead inevitably to birth and rebirth.

At the end of the story, through vision blurred by the loss of her glasses, Hulga watches Manley leave. "When she turned her churning face toward the opening, she saw his blue figure struggling successfully over the green speckled lake."[42] These are traditional colors of the Church—blue associated with the Virgin Mary and spiritual love, and green, the color of hope and fecundity. The gospel, somehow, has broken through the obscene. Manley has discovered that even when he thinks he has found a true heretic, she turns out to have been attracted not to evil and sin, but to innocence and grace. As he leaves, he enacts an archetypal pattern and becomes a Wandering Jew figure, condemned to tell his story over and over again. One knows he will take his contradictory, and yet complementary, messages of sin and gospel with him on a never-ending journey.

Hulga is left lame and immobile, but she has had a vision of something beyond herself, something transcendent that exists in even the possibility of a relationship with someone else. Though it is not love that she has experienced with Manley, it is certainly more than the Nothing she has worshiped before. Although it is dusty, Joy does sit in the sunlight (Sonlight) at the end.

Recall that when she dressed for her rendezvous, she could not find any perfume, and so she rubbed Vapex on her collar, a gesture with not only comic but pathetic dimensions. Perfume can be an instrument of seduction, but Vapex hardly qualifies. Fragrance also has religious significance, for incense carries prayers to heaven. Though she does not possess perfume, she knows it would be appropriate for the occasion. What a contrast, finally, with her mother and Mrs. Freeman pulling onions in the final paragraph—earth-bound, dirty and "evil-smelling."

"The Life You Save May Be Your Own," published two years earlier than "Good Country People," was in some respects O'Connor's practice ground for many of the themes and images in the later story. In both stories a stranger enters the home of a mother and daughter and ultimately deceives and abandons the daughter. In both stories the heart carries a significant symbolic load. When Mrs. Crater asks Mr. Shiftlet where he is from, his response seems evasive. He says, " 'Lady, . . . lemme tell you something. There's one of these doctors in Atlanta that's

taken a knife and cut the human heart—the human heart . . . out
of a man's chest and held it in his hand,' and he held his hand
out, palm up, as if it were slightly weighted with the human
heart, 'and studied it like it was a day-old chicken, and lady,' he
said, allowing a long significant pause in which his head slid
forward and his clay-colored eyes brightened, 'he don't know
no more about it than you or me.' "[43] Shiftlet's identity is contained in the image of the heart more than in his physical birth-
place. He is profoundly touched by the mystery of human existence and identity and the limitations of science in explaining
those mysteries.

Again the fig, symbol of fertility and often used in iconography
in place of the apple tree, also appears in both stories. In "The
Life You Save May Be Your Own" the "fat yellow moon appeared
in the branches of the fig tree as if it were going to roost there
with the chickens."[44] In addition, the sun, which was so significant in the last paragraph of "Good Country People," appears
here often in conjunction with the moon. The sun and moon
together are traditional references to the mourning of all creation
at Christ's crucifixion.[45] Shiftlet himself strikes a peculiar crucifixion pose as he enters Lucynell Crater's yard.

> The tramp stood looking at her and didn't answer. He turned
> his back and faced the sunset. He swung both his whole and
> his short arm up slowly so that they indicated an expanse of
> sky and his figure formed a crooked cross. The old woman
> watched him with her arms folded across her chest as if she
> were the owner of the sun, and the daughter watched, her
> head thrust forward and her fat helpless hands hanging at
> the wrists. She had long pink-gold hair and eyes as blue as a
> peacock's neck . . . . He held the pose for almost fifty sec-
> onds . . . ."[46]

This emblem draws particular attention to itself in its dramatic, photographic, and symbolic presentation. In it is the tramp who faces the sun (the Son) in an attitude of worship and adoration, the old woman who, even though she can look at the sun only through shaded eyes,[47] feels she owns it, and the retarded daughter, whose peacock blue eyes shine as iconographic signs of the Nativity and immortality. In added intensity, the action is stopped for fifty seconds, a breathless moment in the forward moving action of the story.

From the beginning Shiftlet's eyes are on Mrs. Crater's car. He works on it until he has fixed it, he sleeps in it at night, and he marries Lucynell in order to obtain it, yet after the marriage ceremony, Shiftlet feels uncomfortable and dissatisfied.

> As they came out of the courthouse, Mr. Shiftlet began twisting his neck in his collar. He looked morose and bitter as if he had been insulted while someone held him. "That didn't satisfy me none," he said. "That was just something a woman in an office did, nothing but paper work and blood tests. What do they know about my blood? If they was to take my heart and cut it out," he said, "they wouldn't know a thing about me. It didn't satisfy me at all."
>
> "It satisfied the law," the old woman said sharply.
>
> "The law," Mr. Shiftlet said and spit. "It's the law that don't satisfy me."[48]

The law is not enough for Shiftlet because he recognizes that he is using the law to break the law. After he leaves Lucynell asleep at the restaurant on their "honeymoon" journey, he is "more depressed than ever,"[49] and looks for a hitchhiker to fill the silence. Through the windshield the sun is once again shining straight into Shiftlet's face and at the side of the road stands a young boy with a suitcase. Shiftlet stops to pick him up and realizes at once that the boy is running away from home, as he once did himself. Having just abandoned Lucynell, Shiftlet is no one to lecture another on responsibility, but he sees only the mote in the boy's eye and not the log in his own. Shiftlet's mother and Lucynell, whom the cook in the restaurant said looked like an "angel of Gawd," become one person for Shiftlet and he unwittingly speaks the truth about himself:

> "My mother was a angel of Gawd," Mr. Shiftlet said in a very strained voice. "He took her from heaven and giver to me and I left her." His eyes were instantly clouded over with a mist of tears. The car was barely moving.[50]

After the boy tells him to "go to the devil" and jumps out of the car, Shiftlet drives along slowly with the door still open. The weather changes and a cloud appears both in front of him and behind him. He prays, "Oh Lord! . . . Break forth and wash the slime from this earth." At that moment the storm begins and the rear of his car is splattered with rain. It sounds like "tin-can tops"—an appropriate simile for a honeymoon car. Mr. Shiftlet is indeed being pursued by the Lord, and like Ruller in "The Turkey," he is not at all certain that he can outrun Him. He had claimed earlier to have "a moral intelligence."[51] At the end of the story, as he races the rain to Mobile, he has begun to see that *he* is the "slime." His moral intelligence has begun to assert itself.

Earlier in the story, Mr. Shiftlet had asked Mrs. Crater some pointed questions.

> He leaned back against the two-by-four that helped support the porch roof. "Lady," he said slowly, "there's some men that some things mean more to them than money." The old woman rocked without comment and the daughter watched the trigger that moved up and down in his neck. He told the old woman then that all most people were interested in was money, but he asked what a man was made for. He asked her

if a man was made for money, or what. He asked her what
she thought she was made for but she didn't answer, she only
sat rocking and wondered if a one-armed man could put a
new roof on her garden house. He asked a lot of questions
that she didn't answer.[52]

Shiftlet is asking catechetical questions which demand answers, even though at this point he is not yet ready for them.
In "The Enduring Chill" the priest stands over the sick boy and
drills him on the catechism. Shiftlet asks the question the priest
is able to answer: "Why did God make you?" he yells at the boy.
"God made you to know Him, to love Him, to serve Him in this
world and to be happy with Him in the next!"[53] In the hitchhiker's
actions he has confronted himself. He preaches the law of responsibility to the boy, but the law doesn't satisfy. It simply serves
to convict—and the person it convicts is he. It is the first step
to salvation. By the beginning of the storm, Shiftlet seems well
on his way to coming up with the right answers himself.

In "The Comforts of Home," Thomas must likewise run up
against the law before his eyes are opened. Like Hulga-Joy,
another homebound intellectual in her thirties, Thomas sees
clearly what is wrong with his mother, but cannot see the irony
in his diagnosis of her ills, which actually identifies his own
spiritual illness. He complains that she made "a mockery of
virtue . . . pursue[d] it with such a mindless intensity that
everyone involved was made a fool of and virtue itself became
ridiculous."[54] His mother's offending virtue is that she has had
released from jail Sarah Ham, an unregenerate floozy, a bad-
check writer, and a drunk, and has taken her into her own home,
against the wishes of her son. Thomas considers Sarah a "moral
moron," and naturally he believes that she does not belong in
his comfortable, orderly territory. When she finds her way to his
bed, he is outraged and backs her out of the room and down
the hall with a chair, like a lion-tamer.

The virtuous man wards off the lure of sin, as if it were a beast which must be kept at bay. But in this emblem, Thomas does not recognize his own depravity. He considers himself a moral being, but virtue is for Thomas merely a "principle of order," a way of keeping the surface calm. The mother does not relent. She keeps saying to him, "I keep thinking [Sarah Ham] might be you." The idea completely revolts Thomas, even though at one point he feels "a deep unbearable loathing for himself as if he were turning slowly into the girl."[55] The girl herself picks up on this theme, complaining, after he shoves her out of his car, "What if you were me and I couldn't stand to ride you three miles?"[56] Thomas sees only "blameless corruption" in the girl, whose behavior psychologists have explained with the lingo O'Connor found so repugnant. The girl is labelled a nymphomaniac and a congenital liar, suffering from "insecurities." These psychological labels the girl herself throws around, using them as excuses for her actions. She is a creature who takes no responsibility for her own behavior.

Thomas's problem, like that of so many of O'Connor's characters, is that he sees clearly only half of the truth, the law which condemns, and he sees it only as it applies to others. He does not realize that this same law is fulfilled by the gospel, nor does he recognize his own need for salvation. He does not seem to be aware, at least on a conscious level, that the law which condemns Sarah Ham also condemns him. He is not separate from the law.

In this story O'Connor seems to be hearing echoes from Paul's letter to the Romans where he sets forth the alternatives: "Let not sin therefore reign in your mortal bodies, to make you obey their passions. Do not yield your members to sin as instruments of wickedness . . . ." Thomas understands this much. He lives an upright life and expects others in his household to do likewise. But the passage continues: ". . . but yield yourselves to God as men who have been brought from death to life, and your members to God as instruments of righteousness. For sin will have no dominion over you, since you are not under law but under grace" (Romans 6:12-14, RSV). Thomas's god, the one who gives him direction, is his dead father. And his father, really a devil figure, gives him no freedom from the law, but burdens him with his condemnations. "Idiot," the father calls the son, and "moron" and "imbecile" and "fool." Thomas, impotent by himself, haunted by the image of his father, is completely captive to this ghost. There is no grace here.

Paul's words in Romans 7:4-6 assume ironic significance when read in the light of Thomas's dilemma. "Likewise, my brethren, you have died to the law through the body of Christ, so that you may belong to another, to him who has been raised from the dead in order that we may bear fruit for God" (RSV). Thomas belongs to another, who seems to have returned from the dead to direct him, but this one certainly bears no fruit for God. In fact, the father represents the opposite of everything the mother stands for. The passage continues: "While we were living in the flesh, our sinful passions, aroused by the law, were at work in our members to bear fruit for death. But now we are discharged from the law, dead to that which held us captive, so that we serve not under the old written code but in the new life of the Spirit." There is no new life for Thomas, for he has not yet encountered the Spirit.

Ironically, it is the "schoolmaster" of the law which finally points the way for Thomas. Paul writes, "If it had not been for the law, I should not have known sin." Thomas must finally recognize himself as a fellow laborer under the law, a sinner like the rest of mankind, something he seems to have known only subliminally before, in the momentary flash of recognition which overtakes him as he rails against the girl.

At the end of the story he literally stands with a smoking gun, his mother dead. As the sheriff peers around the corner of the door, he sees "over her body, the killer and the slut . . . about to collapse into each other's arms." The law here, represented by the sheriff, actually catches and condemns Thomas, but Thomas has already seen the connection between himself and Sarah Ham. He has recognized his entry into the ranks of sinners. Now perhaps he can be saved.

The first step toward grace in Paul's writings and in O'Connor's stories must be the conviction of one's sins. Only the most violent crime—matricide—will shake Thomas into this consciousness. He is not only an ordinary sinner, he is a murderer. O'Connor stops here. We are not allowed to see any transformation in Thomas. In other stories she will fully develop the theme of law and gospel, but here she allows us only the brief, final glimpse of one man's awakening to his own depravity. The awakening is essential, for until it occurs he will never recognize his desperate need for the gospel.

— 3 —

Discharged from the Law

How *should the gospel inform the writing of the Christian novelist?* Flannery O'Connor gives a plain answer. The writer who is thoroughly Christian will be unable to write anything without in some way revealing God. This is not to say that "message" should ever be slapped on top of story—like jam on bread. Rather, God is in the loaf itself.

In "Catholic Novelists and Their Readers" O'Connor says, "The novelist doesn't write to express himself, he doesn't write simply to render a vision he believes true, rather he renders his vision so that it can be transferred, as nearly whole as possible, to his reader . . . . The sorry religious novel comes about when the writer supposes that because of his belief, he is somehow dispensed from the obligation to penetrate concrete reality."[1] The gospel in no way restricts the novelist; rather it broadens the world the novelist must portray. The artistic difficulty lies in making revelatory action believable to the modern reader, for whom grace is what is mumbled hastily once a year before the Thanksgiving meal. In a review of Caroline Gordon's *The Malefactors*, O'Connor contended that "a novel dealing with a conver-

sion is the most difficult the fiction writer can assign himself . . . . Making grace believable to the contemporary reader
is the almost insurmountable problem of the novelist who writes
from the standpoint of Christian orthodoxy."[2]

Again, the emblem becomes an appropriate metaphor for describing O'Connor's aesthetics, and one finds that the closer and
more prolonged her characters' encounters with the divine, the
more frequently she uses this emblematic technique. "Parker's
Back," one of O'Connor's last stories, is one of her most visual
and most emblematic.

The story is really about the encounter of law and gospel.
Sarah Ruth Cates, one of the plainest women in literature, is
bony and judgmental. There is nothing soft about her or her
belief, which is legalistic and arbitrary. She does not approve of
automobiles, tobacco, whiskey, profanity, make-up, churches
(they're idolatrous), or color of any kind. But she is drawn inexplicably to O.E. Parker, who arrives in a truck, is tattooed from
head to foot and yells profanities as an introduction.

Much to O.E.'s surprise, he is also attracted to her, even though
her immediate response to his profanity is a swift broom-beating.
This mysterious attraction echoes his fascination with the tattooed man at the circus many years before, and foreshadows the
mystery of his later attraction to Christ. What seems to engage
his interest in Sarah Ruth is her obvious connection with something other than herself. O. E., in his initially hazy understanding
of the transcendent, thinks Sarah Ruth is Christian, whereas
what Sarah Ruth represents is the swift, retaliatory action of the
law. Later, when O.E. suggests she climb in the back of his truck
with him, she pushes him out of the truck door. Her response
to the suggestion of sin is swift and merciless.

But her vision is clouded. When O.E. asks her which is her
favorite tattoo, she points to an eagle and calls it a chicken.
Significantly, the eagle is a traditional symbol of the resurrection
and the cock is Peter's symbol of betrayal. What the reader is to

discover is that while Sarah Ruth seems to understand and represent law and judgment, she allows no sense of the transcendent
or the sacramental in her theology. She does not infuse the concrete realities of this world with any spiritual significance at all.
Worse, her ultimate denial that God appeared in human form
declares her a heretic.

Parker, on the other hand, smothers his skin with sign and
symbol. He is after the same sense of the transcendent and the
mysterious that he received when, early in his life, he watched
a tattooed man at a circus.

> Except for his loins which were girded with a panther hide,
> the man's skin was patterned in what seemed from Parker's
> distance—he was near the back of the tent, standing on a
> bench—a single intricate design of brilliant color. The man,
> who was small and sturdy, moved about on the platform,
> flexing his muscles so that the arabesque of men and beasts
> and flowers on his skin appeared to have a subtle motion of
> its own. Parker was filled with emotion, lifted up as some
> people are when the flag passes.[3]

Parker wants to participate in this artistic, even theological
moment himself, but he discovers that after he has had almost
his entire body tattooed—all except his back—the effect is not
the same. His tattoos have no unity. Arranged haphazardly and
incongruently, they do not move together.

Parker's body, then, becomes one giant emblem of his spiritual
condition. His eagle is on top of a cannon, next to a serpent
coiled around a shield, the symbol of the resurrection positioned
next to the traditional symbol of evil and deceit, which is twisted
around a shield, reminiscent of Paul's shield of faith with which
the Christian is to "quench all the flaming darts of the evil one"
(Ephesians 6:16, RSV). To complicate matters further, between
the tattoos of the eagle and the serpent are hearts, some of which

are pierced, a traditional sign of contrition and repentance. In addition, his tattoos include his mother's name on a heart, anchors (early Christian symbols for salvation and the cross), crossed rifles, a tiger (Blakean?), a panther, a cobra coiled about a torch (another symbol for Christ as the light of the world), a deck of cards, hawks on his thighs and obscenities on his belly. Of course, Parker cannot know that he has created incompatible dichotomies. All he feels is a nameless dissatisfaction.

Like Jonah (to whom O'Connor compares him later in the bar), Parker runs away from God when his mother tries to get him to go to church with her. He is not interested. In fact, he is terrified and goes off to join the Navy, hiding himself in the belly of "the gray mechanical ship,"[4] just as Jonah hid himself until God delivered him into the belly of the whale.

After Parker marries Sarah Ruth, his dissatisfaction becomes so great that he decides that perhaps he will have his unmarked back tattooed, even though in the past he has not liked anything he could not see (a contrast to Sarah Ruth whose theology will admit nothing visible). Parker looks for a religious subject, one which will appeal to Sarah Ruth. God, however, gets to Parker before he can decide on an appropriate picture for his back. Parker has already decided that he needs something better than the Bible for his back. For Parker the word of God is not going to be enough. Finally, only the Word of God—that is, Jesus Christ—will do.

The central emblematic moment, the moment when law and gospel meet in this story, is when Parker is knocked off his tractor by the cross. The old woman for whom he is working has warned him not to hit the tree in the middle of the field.

> Parker began at the outside of the field and made circles inward toward it. He had to get off the tractor every now and then and untangle the baling cord or kick a rock out of the way. The old woman had told him to carry the rocks to the

edge of the field, which he did when she was there watching. When he thought he could make it, he ran over them. As he circled the field his mind was on a suitable design for his back. The sun, the size of a golf ball, began to switch regularly from in front to behind him, but he appeared to see it both places as if he had eyes in the back of his head. All at once he saw the tree reaching out to grasp him. A ferocious thud propelled him into the air, and he heard himself yelling in an unbelievably loud voice, "GOD ABOVE!"

The circles Parker makes are motions of completion, an ancient sign of the eternal. In this passage the motion is inward, the movement of God bringing Parker closer and closer. Hypnotized as the sun shifts "from in front to behind him . . . he appeared to see it both places as if he had eyes in the back of his head," and he runs smack into the tree.

But notice that the tree seems to reach out for him. (Recall Ruller in "The Turkey," lying sprawled on the ground, having run into God.) Appropriately, Parker's first response is to yell, "God above." It is God above who has knocked him off that tractor, who has blinded him with His sun (Son), and who now has even taken away his shoes.[5] The emblem here is Parker as a barefoot Moses, standing next to the burning bush. "The first thing Parker saw were his shoes, quickly being eaten by the fire; one was caught under the tractor, the other was some distance away, burning by itself. He was not in them. He could feel the hot breath of the burning tree on his face. He scrambled backwards, still sitting, his eyes cavernous, and if he had known how to cross himself he would have done it."[6]

Parker has been forced to confront his own mortality. He has come close to death, and in its proximity, has come close to God. He realizes that a tremendous change has occurred in him, and he also realizes that it is not necessarily going to be easy for him from now on. It is now "a leap forward into a worse unknown."[7]

This is a hard reality, this Christ. He rushes to the tattooist to respond in the only way he knows.

After he has chosen the Byzantine Christ for his back, Parker goes to the Haven of Light Christian Mission where he is given, appropriately, a new pair of shoes and is kept awake all night by the light from the neon cross. This cross will keep him from sleeping and will lead the next day to greater agonies. His first response on looking at the artist's painting of Christ on his back is to drink a full pint of whiskey in five minutes. The tattoo leads to a fight in the bar he usually frequents, and when he returns home, it leads to a further separation from Sarah Ruth. Parker is discovering that while his dissatisfaction is disappearing, he has also lost his ability to live the same life he has always lived. He has changed. For good.

Obadiah Elihue, having accepted the gospel in a way which he will never be able to forget, is now attacked by the law. Sarah Ruth hones in on his sinfulness, reminding him of his lies to her about the "hefty blonde" he worked for, who, she has discovered, is really an old woman. And then Parker, completely unprepared for her response, reveals to her the Christ on his back. She does not recognize the face.

In fact, she denies Christ entirely, saying that God is a spirit only, and Parker, suffering again under the lashes of her broom, is thrashed for the Christ on his back and for his sinfulness. But Parker's back is now Christ's face, and the welts, rising redly on one, also disfigure the other. The bond between the two is irrevocable and Parker's only comfort now is the supreme comfort—that he has a tree, a cross, to lean on, that in his suffering he experiences only what Christ himself felt. The spirit of utter mutuality and unity, what his tattoos have always up to now lacked—descends on him and he realizes the terrible cost. The Word has become flesh on his own flesh.

Flannery O'Connor said, in defending her use of violence in her stories, "When you can assume that your audience holds the same beliefs you do, you can relax a little and use more normal means of talking to it; when you have to assume that it does not, then you have to make your vision apparent by shock— to the hard of hearing you shout, and for the almost-blind you draw large and startling figures."[8] "Parker's Back" is filled with these emblematic, large, and startling figures: the tattoos themselves, the hand of God in the form of a tree reaching out to grab Parker from his seat on the tractor, the burning tree, the face of Christ staring at the places Parker has just been, the face of Christ beaten by Sarah Ruth. O'Connor is using emblem and allegory in their most imaginative and sophisticated forms to tell the story of a twentieth-century pilgrim's progress.

In "The Lame Shall Enter First" Rufus Johnson, a juvenile delinquent with a club foot and an IQ of 140, becomes the informing emblem. Another version of The Misfit in "A Good Man Is Hard to Find," Johnson has confessed his belief in God's free grace, recognized the power of Satan in his life, and deliberately chosen evil. But he sees the truth and preaches it to Norton, the young and neglected son of a social worker, ironically named Sheppard.

Sheppard is a good man. As his son says, "He helps people."[9] But Johnson knows that good works are never sufficient. "I don't care if he's good or not," he says. "He ain't right." Sheppard also does not understand love, without which his good works are ineffectual. His wife dead a year, he cannot comprehend his son Norton's grief, which he considers excessive. Unable to satisfy his child's emotional needs, he is also predictably unable to provide the proper physical nourishment for himself and his son.

The story opens with an emblem: Sheppard eating soggy cereal out of a cardboard box, and Norton cutting himself a piece of chocolate cake, spreading it with peanut butter and ketchup—a concoction which, to the disgust of his father, he vomits up. Completely blind to his child's predicament, the father tells him about Rufus Johnson, whom he discovered the day before going through garbage pails in search of his dinner. Sheppard decides that his own son, who has so much, would benefit from sharing what he does have with one "less fortunate," so Rufus Johnson comes to live with them. The irony is that Rufus understands good nourishment, and he also understands just who is the more and who is the less fortunate. His first meal, which he orders the child to prepare for him, consists of a sandwich, milk and an orange. Furthermore, what Rufus Johnson does is not so much accept charity from Sheppard, as share what he knows— the gospel—with the hungry and the poor in spirit—Norton.

In an emblematic scene at the dinner table, Sheppard laughs at Rufus's belief in Scripture and ridicules him, saying, "You don't believe it. You're too intelligent." Rufus responds saying, "I ain't too intelligent . . . . You don't know nothing about me. Even if I didn't believe it, it would still be true." He opens the Scriptures, tears out a page, chews it up and swallows it. "I've eaten it like Ezekiel," he says, "and it was honey to my mouth."[10] Rufus has found true nourishment.[11] This does not make him a better person in Sheppard's eyes.

Rather than respond with love and concern for Rufus, Sheppard begins to hate him. He has had ideas of educating the boy, exposing him to astronomy, giving him a vision for his future. In an attempt to engage Rufus's curiosity, he has bought a telescope and installed it in his attic. Ironically, it is his own child, Norton, whom he has considered dull and uneducable, who becomes fascinated with the telescope. Rufus has told the child that since his mother believed in Jesus, she was saved and is now "on high . . . in the sky somewhere . . . but you got to be dead to get there."[12] The child has spent hours gazing through the telescope, attempting to find her, which he finally succeeds in doing, and reports to his father, who ignores him.

After Rufus Johnson is arrested for a final time, Sheppard's blindness is stripped away. He begins to rationalize, and ends by seeing the horrible truth about himself.

> "I have nothing to reproach myself with," he repeated. His voice sounded dry and harsh. "I did more for him than I did for my own child." He was swept with a sudden panic. He heard the boy's jubilant voice. Satan has you in his power . . . . He heard his voice as if it were the voice of his accuser . . . . The sentence echoed in his mind, each syllable like a dull blow. His mouth twisted and he closed his eyes against the revelation.[13]

He sees himself clearly for the first time, and he is revolted. Picking up the emblem of eating with which the story began, O'Connor writes that "he had stuffed his own emptiness with good works like a glutton. He had ignored his own child to feed his vision of himself." He feels "a rush of agonizing love for the child," and he runs to find him, but it is too late. The child is hanging from the rafters of the attic, having joined his mother at the other end of the telescope.

Sarah Ruth in "Parker's Back" is an old-fashioned heretic of the gnostic strain, viewing Christ as non-corporeal. In contrast, Sheppard is the modern agnostic whose faith in education and in good works provides a vague and clichéd system of values. He says to his child, "Listen . . . your mother's spirit lives on in other people and it'll live on in you if you're good and generous like she was."[14] But both Sarah Ruth and Sheppard share an inability to see God in concrete, human form—in particular in the Incarnation. For both of them the result of this deficiency is that they are unable to give or receive love. Sarah Ruth, one feels, will never see clearly. For Sheppard, there is more hope, although he has been forced in a particularly horrible way to face the results of his self-absorbed behavior. Finally, however, he is forced to recognize the light of his child's face, "the image of his salvation." Discharged from the law of good works, he rushes in love to respond to his child—the love creating the desire for a new kind of good work in his life—that produced by his love of others rather than his love of himself. But he is too late. The child, who has long been "discharged from the law," teaches his father the meaning of death which he did not learn when his wife died. Again violence, death, and revelation are linked.

Occasionally, O'Connor deals more gently with her characters. In one of her favorite stories, "The Artificial Nigger," a grandfather and his grandson take a mythic journey from the country into the city, discovering the truth about love and God's mercy. Frederick Asals has observed that this story "fully exhibits [O'Connor's] mature sacramentalism, that double vision which seeks to use imagery both literally and symbolically."[15] The story begins and ends with an emblematic scene linking moonlight and God's grace. The moon, silver and beautiful, pours its "dignifying light" on the room Mr. Head shares with his grandson, Nelson. The moonlight transforms the room, creating brocade out of pillow ticking, silver out of the wooden floor boards, and even giving Mr. Head's trousers "an almost noble air, like the garment some great man had just flung to his servant . . . ."[16] The emphasis is on nobility, dignity, even royalty. Mr. Head "might have been Vergil summoned in the middle of the night to go to Dante, or better, Raphael, awakened by a blast of God's light to fly to the side of Tobias."[17] His mission, accompanying the child on a revelatory journey, is sacred, mystical, archetypal. While the journey functions as a type of initiation rite for the child, it provides an even more important experience for Mr. Head. He is a man of excellent intentions, but great pride. "His physical reactions, like his moral ones, were guided by his will and strong character. . . . [He felt] entirely confident that he could carry out the moral mission of the coming day"[18]—to show

"Wake Me Up In Time To Clap!"

Cartoon originally published in "Colonnade," volume XVIII, no. 26, p. 2, April 17, 1943, Georgia College, Milledgeville, Georgia.

Nelson the evils of the city and instill in him a desire never to leave home again.

Mr. Head has a natural penchant for allegory, conceiving the journey in moral terms.[19] "It was to be a lesson that the boy would never forget. He was to find out from it that he had no cause for pride merely because he had been born in a city." Once they arrive in Atlanta, Mr. Head tells Nelson in a heavily allegorical gesture to squat down and stick his head in the sewer.

> Then Mr. Head explained the sewer system, how the entire city was underlined with it, how it contained all the drainage and was full of rats and how a man could slide into it and be sucked along down endless pitchblack tunnels. At any minute any man in the city might be sucked into the sewer and never heard from again. He described it so well that Nelson was for some seconds shaken. He connected the sewer passages with the entrance to hell and understood for the first time how the world was put together in its lower parts.[20]

In preparation for the long day, Mr. Head packs a lunch of bread and fish, reminiscent of the loaves and fishes Christ used for the feeding of the five thousand. In the confusion of the arrival into Atlanta, however, the grandfather forgets the lunch, leaving it on the train. This will not, the reader realizes, be a day of quick and easy nourishment. The message of salvation has a stronger appeal to those who are hungry and suffering, as Mr. Head will be later. He will encounter God in the midst of his own agony.

Early in the day Nelson learns the lesson his grandfather wants to teach him. During the first part of the trip his feelings toward his grandfather change in stages from shame, to cockiness, to gratitude. But it does not take much to convince him of his dependency on his grandfather: "He realized the old man would be his only support in the strange place they were approaching. He would be entirely alone in the world if he were ever lost from his grandfather. A terrible excitement shook him and he wanted to take hold of Mr. Head's coat and hold on like a child."[21] This is exactly where Mr. Head wants him—physically and emotionally—but Mr. Head has his own lessons to learn. "Have you ever seen me lost?"[22] he asks the boy at one point. The fact is that Mr. Head must be lost before he can be found, and he will spend much of the day in apparently directionless wandering in the big city before God's mercy finally finds him.

There is also an early indication that Mr. Head is not in as much control as he thinks he is. He awakens early and plans to rise before Nelson does, so he can fix breakfast and have it waiting for him. As it turns out, Mr. Head falls back asleep and awakens to the smell of frying fatback. Nelson is dressed and the breakfast he has cooked is ready.

In the city Nelson gains the upper hand in a painful episode in which his grandfather publicly denies knowing him. It is not long before Mr. Head knows he has made a terrible mistake. Nelson follows him at a distance now, refusing water, refusing to speak. They have lost their way and Mr. Head imagines the fate that is awaiting them. Beaten and robbed, they will be completely alone in the dark of the city. "The speed of God's justice was only what he expected for himself, but he could not stand to think that his sins would be visited upon Nelson and that even now, he was leading the boy to his doom."[23] Furthermore, Mr. Head is convinced that now the pattern has been established, that he is "wandering into a black strange place where nothing was like it had ever been before, a long old age, without respect and an end that would be welcome because it would be the end." Nelson, meanwhile, follows blankly, "his mind . . . frozen around his grandfather's treachery as if he were trying to preserve it intact to present at the final judgment."[24]

Mr. Head has sinned and fallen short of the glory of God—and it is this recognition that propels him forward to seek help. "Oh Gawd I'm lost!" he yells to a passerby, and he receives help in the form of directions to the nearest train station. He moves forward mechanically, not really caring about anything now: "He felt he knew now what time would be like without seasons and what heat would be like without light and what man would be like without salvation." Locked inside a system of law and judgment, feeling no forgiveness from Nelson, he is completely trapped.

But then the central emblem of the story appears: the "artificial nigger"—a statue attached with putty to the top of a wall. It is in this unlikely object that Mr. Head finds the gospel, for the artificial nigger has attributes similar to both Nelson and Mr. Head. To begin with, "it was not possible to tell if the artificial Negro were meant to be young or old." Throughout the story O'Connor has reminded us of the close identification between the grandfather and the grandchild. Mr. Head is described as an "ancient child" and Nelson as a "miniature old man." The statue is "about Nelson's size," and it is "pitched forward at an unsteady angle," similar to the boy and the old man who stand "with their necks forward at almost the same angle and their shoulders curved in almost exactly the same way."

The grandfather names the statue and Nelson repeats the phrase, and they stand entranced, as if in front of a "great mystery, some monument to another's victory . . . [bringing] them together in their common defeat." They are attracted to the misery they see in the emblem-icon—and the suffering which they now share. They are, in a real sense, at the foot of the cross of the suffering Christ, feeling both agony and mercy.[25] The experience of encountering the "artificial nigger" brings the boy and the man together, restores the old man's dignity, and reawakens the boy's respect for his grandfather.

As the train leaves them at the country stop, the moon silvers the landscape once again.

Mr. Head stood very still and felt the action of mercy touch him again but this time he knew that there were no words in the world that could name it. He understood that it grew out of agony, which is not denied to any man and which is given in strange ways to children. He understood it was all a man could carry into death to give his Maker and he suddenly burned with shame that he had so little of it to take with him. He stood appalled, judging himself with the thoroughness of God, while the action of mercy covered his pride like a flame and consumed it.[26]

Judged by the standards of the law, he realizes his miserable failure, but next to the judgment of God, he also feels for the first time, mercy and forgiveness, so that he is loosed from the law's terrible claim on him. He is both condemned and saved, and "since God loved in proportion as He forgave, he felt ready at that instant to enter Paradise."

Some remarkable echoes of this story are found in Isaiah 30, a chapter in which the Israelites are warned against an alliance with Egypt. The chapter begins with words that could be taken straight from Mr. Head's mouth: "Woe to the rebellious children, saith the Lord, that take counsel, but not of me." Mr. Head will, of course, realize that he, too, is a rebellious child—maybe even more so than Nelson. These children "walk to go down into Egypt" in spite of God's counsel, even though Egypt feels nothing but shame and embarrassment about them, "a people that could not profit them." These children are "the burden of the beasts of the south," and prefer lies to the truth of God's prophecy. (Recall the "fortunes" Nelson and Mr. Head receive from the weighing machine.) Judgment, God warns, will come to these children, "as a breach ready to fall, swelling out in a high wall, whose breaking cometh suddenly at an instant." The wall on which the "artificial nigger" is balanced does not break, but the image and the revelation that accompany it break through to Mr. Head immediately.

The old man and boy return from Egypt-Atlanta to their Paradise, their enclosed garden.[27] As Nelson says, "I'm glad I've went once, but I'll never go back again!"[28] complying with Isaiah's admonition that "in returning and rest shall ye be saved." Meanwhile, God waits, "that he may be gracious unto you, and therefore will he be exalted, that he may have mercy upon you: for the LORD is a god of judgment: blessed are all they that wait for him." Here is Mr. Head's God of judgment and of mercy. Even while the old man was lost in the labyrinth of city streets, turning left many times at first, and later losing track of his left and right turns, God was there. As Isaiah says, "And thine ears shall hear a word behind thee, saying, This is the way, walk ye in it, when ye turn to the right hand, and when ye turn to the left."

The final verses of Isaiah 30 complement the final paragraphs of "The Artificial Nigger." Isaiah says, "The light of the moon shall be as the light of the sun." O'Connor's moon "sprang from a cloud and flooded the clearing with light . . . the white clouds illuminated like lanterns." Nature is transfigured as God blesses and heals. In fact, Mr. Head feels "the action of mercy cover[ing] his pride like a flame and consum[ing] it," paralleling Jehovah in Isaiah who "shall cause his glorious voice to be heard, and shall show the lighting down of his arm, with the indignation of his anger, and with the flame of a devouring fire. . . ."

The train disappears "like a frightened serpent into the woods."[29] The challenge has been met and accepted. Mr. Head has received revelation and salvation. He has been discharged from the law into grace.

— 4 —

Sacrament:
The Outward and Visible Sign

In an address delivered to a symposium at Sweetbriar College, O'Connor contended that "the real novelist, the one with an instinct for what he is about, knows that he cannot approach the infinite directly, that he must penetrate the natural human world as it is. The more sacramental his theology, the more encouragement he will get from it to do just that."[1] The sacramentalist is anchored in the concrete world—and the source of that anchoring is the Incarnation, God as historical person, God as a sensory entity, God rooted in human experience. The sacramentalist views the things of this world as vehicles for God's grace. As Frederick Asals has explained O'Connor's sacramentalism, "It is the natural world that becomes the vehicle of the supernatural, and her characters' literal return to their senses becomes the means of opening their imaginations to receive it."[2] The emblems and their accompanying symbols in O'Connor's work force the characters' (and the readers') attention to an immediately apprehendable truth—approachable because it is grounded in everyday reality and can be experienced through the eyes and the ears.

The emblems begin with the first sentence of "The Displaced

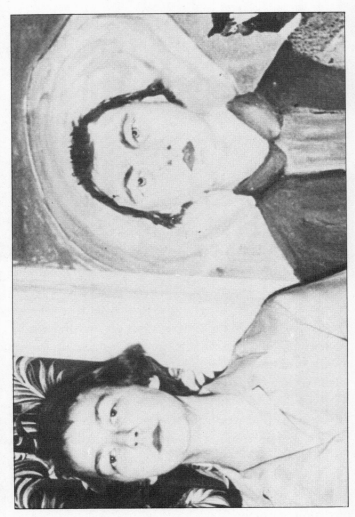

Flannery O'Connor and self-portrait with peacock

O'Connor Collection, Ina Dillard Russell Library, Georgia College, Milledgeville, Georgia

Person": "The peacock was following Mrs. Shortley up the road to the hill where she meant to stand."[3] The peacock is one of O'Connor's most symbolically resonant figures. Because of its firm flesh, which was thought not to decay, the peacock appears often in iconography as a symbol of the Resurrection, particularly when its feathers are spread. In addition, the "eyes" in the feathers were thought to represent either God's omniscience or the Church's eternal presence. So in "The Displaced Person" when Mrs. Shortley is followed very closely by a peacock, the implication is that God is in pursuit. Mrs. Shortley, however, is indifferent, keeping her back to the bird.

Furthermore, "she ignored the white afternoon sun which was creeping behind a ragged wall of cloud as if it pretended to be an intruder and cast her gaze down the red clay road that turned off from the highway."[4] Here again is the pervasive sun/Son connection. Mrs. Shortley's attention is focused on neither the transcendent, nor the Church, nor God, nor Christ, but rather on the red clay road, the earth. She stands "on two tremendous legs, with the grand self-confidence of a mountain, and [rises], up narrowing bulges of granite, to two icy blue points of light that [pierce] forward, surveying everything," reminiscent of the ruins of Ozymandias's statue in Shelley's poem of the same name. Shelley's sculpture has "two vast and trunkless legs of stone" and:

> . . . Near them, on the sand,
> Half sunk, a shattered visage lies, whose frown,
> And wrinkled lip, and sneer of cold command,
> Tell that its sculptor well those passions read
> Which yet survive, stamped on these lifeless things,
> The hand that mocked them, and the heart that fed;
> And on the pedestal these words appear:
> "My name is Ozymandias, king of kings:
> Look on my works, ye Mighty, and despair!"
> Nothing beside remains. Round the decay

Of that colossal wreck, boundless and bare
The lone and level sands stretch far away.[5]

Both the towering Ozymandias and the sculpture built to reflect
his stature exist no more. Mrs. Shortley's days are similarly limited, and she, like Ozymandias, considers neither the irony of
her actions nor her words.

Another statue appears in the story—the statue which Judge
McIntyre had chosen for his grave because it looked so much
like his wife. In yet another variation on the Ozymandias theme,
only the feet of this angel now remain, the rest of the stone
having been chopped and stolen by transient workers. Even
stone, Shelley says, decays, and O'Connor concurs, yet neither
Mrs. McIntyre nor Mrs. Shortley nor Ozymandias seem to recognize the limitations of their human natures. They do recognize
the limitations of everyone else's, however.

The emblem with which the story begins is further developed
in the second paragraph.

The peacock stopped just behind her, his tail—glittering
green-gold and blue in the sunlight—lifted just enough so
that it would not touch the ground. It flowed out on either
side like a floating train and his head on the long blue reed-like
neck was drawn back as if his attention were fixed in the
distance on something no one else could see.[6]

The warm, liquid colors of the bird, the green and blue of regen-
eration and spiritual growth, contrast with Mrs. Shortley's ici-
ness. The peacock's glittering gold, the color of divinity, connects
it with something invisible but compelling, just as the peacock's
gaze is fixed "on something no one else could see."

The emblem of the divine pursuing the human, who doesn't
even recognize its presence, is mirrored in another way by the

priest who arranges for the Poles to work for Mrs. McIntyre. The priest is overcome with awe for the bird.

> "So beauti-ful," the priest said. "A tail full of suns," and he crept forward on tiptoe and looked down on the bird's back where the polished gold and green design began. The peacock stood still as if he had just come down from some sun-drenched height to be a vision for them all. The priest's homely red face hung over him glowing with pleasure.[7]

Mrs. Shortley is not impressed. "Nothing but a peachicken," she mutters, and one is reminded of Sarah Ruth Cates's reaction to Parker's tattoo in "Parker's Back."

> He thrust the arm back at her. "Which you like best?"
> "None of them," she said, "but the chicken is not as bad as the rest."
> "What chicken?" Parker almost yelled.
> She pointed to the eagle.
> "That's an eagle," Parker said. "What fool would waste their time having a chicken put on themself?"[8]

The Poles surprise Mrs. Shortley because, first of all, they look no different from other people. In defining "displaced person" for Astor, she had said that it "means they ain't where they were born at and there's nowhere for them to go—like if you was run out of here and wouldn't nobody have you." These are prophetic words, but as usual Mrs. Shortley sees displacement as something that happens only to others, never to herself. And besides, she thinks, "If they had come from where that kind of thing was done to them, who was to say they were not the kind that would also do it to others?"[9] This perversion of the golden rule becomes the key statement of the story, for before revelation can occur,

Mrs. Shortley has to be divested of her idea that she must do unto others as they have done unto her. As she comes to recognize the commonality of all persons, she will realize that she, too, is a displaced person.

Mrs. Shortley's understanding of Christianity is limited, but when she does consider the Church, she comes up with the usual clichés. Religion for her is nothing more than a social form. She says of her husband, "It is no man that works as hard as Chancey, or is as easy with a cow, or is more of a Christian."[10] If faith exists at all in her, it is works-oriented, which makes it all the more surprising that she is chosen by God to prophesy.

Prophecy comes naturally to her, but she often does not recognize it when it comes and when she does think she has had a vision, she misinterprets it. This is similar to many of John Bunyan's characters, who cannot interpret their emblems correctly in *The Pilgrim's Progress*. When Mrs. McIntyre buys a new silage machine and Mr. Guizac, the Pole, proves his worth by being able to run it efficiently, Mrs. Shortley says that yes, the field might be cut in two days, "if don't no terrible accident occur."[11] The accident does not occur in Mrs. Shortley's lifetime, but when it does occur, it kills Mr. Guizac and ruins Mrs. McIntyre.

Recognizing the Guizacs' threat to her own position, Mrs. Shortley begins to read Scripture, concentrating on the Apocalypse and the Prophets. She begins to see that she is part of a mysterious plan, but once again, she sees only half the truth.

> She saw plainly that the meaning of the world was a mystery that had been planned and she was not surprised to suspect that she had a special part in the plan because she was strong. She saw that the Lord God Almighty had created the strong people to do what had to be done and she felt that she would be ready when she was called.[12]

Mrs. Shortley, ever the misinterpreter, after reading the

prophecies of destruction, takes even more pride in her strength. But she has rather missed the point. The prophets have not awakened her to her vulnerability and her sinfulness; she has instead taken their warnings as applicable to the rest of the world, excluding herself. She has become the only righteous one. The visionary prophecies of Ezekiel have, nonetheless, entered her imagination and, combined with her memory of wartime newsreels, have encouraged her emblematic vision.

> Suddenly while she watched, the sky folded back in two pieces like the curtain to a stage and a gigantic figure stood facing her. It was the color of the sun in the early afternoon, white-gold. It was of no definite shape but there were fiery wheels with fierce dark eyes in them, spinning rapidly all around it. She was not able to tell if the figure was going forward or backward because its magnificence was so great. She shut her eyes in order to look at it and it turned blood-red and the wheels turned white. A voice, very resonant, said the one word, "Prophesy!"
>
> She stood there, tottering slightly but still upright, her eyes shut tight and her fists clenched and her straw sun hat low on her forehead. "The children of wicked nations will be butchered," she said in a loud voice. "Legs where arms should be, foot to face, ear in the palm of hand. Who will remain whole? Who will remain whole? Who?"[13]

Mrs. Shortley had always felt that the Holocaust was something to be expected from uncivilized nations and their "primitive religion," ironic in the face of her own primitive religious practices. In the passage above, her exposure to pictures of the concentration camps combines with an unwitting prophecy of her own death. That she prophesies, however, does not mean that she understands. Soon, in trying to escape her fate (she has overheard Mrs. McIntyre saying she is going to give the Shortleys their thirty days' notice), Mrs. Shortley will meet her real fate, but first she hurriedly packs the family's belongings and they set out before dawn.

> Mrs. Shortley sat with one foot on a packing box so that her knee was pushed into her stomach. Mr. Shortley's elbow was almost under her nose and Sarah Mae's bare foot was sticking over the front seat, touching her ear . . . . [Mrs. Shortley] was sitting in an erect way in spite of the fact that one leg was twisted under and one knee was almost into her neck, but there was a peculiar lack of light in her icy blue eyes. All the vision in them might have been turned around, looking inside her. She suddenly grabbed Mr. Shortley's elbow and Sarah Mae's foot at the same time and began to tug and pull on them as if she were trying to fit the two extra limbs onto herself.[14]

She thus enacts her own prophecy: legs where arms should be, foot to face, ear in the palm of hand. She has not remained whole, but in the process of disintegration, she has received revelation for the first and only time in her life. She has been forced to see the connection between the piles of bodies in the newsreel and herself. In fact, she *becomes* the pile of disconnected body parts. She has been forced, if only very briefly at the moment of death, to see herself as a displaced person, now having "been displaced in the world from all that belonged to her."[15]

So the definition of the displaced person widens to include Mrs. Shortley, but the story is not over yet. Mrs. McIntyre, who believes that with the Guizacs' arrival she has been "saved," must learn the true meaning of salvation. She, unlike Mrs. Shortley, recognizes the worth of Mr. Guizac. "She didn't know anything about him except that he did the work. The truth was that he was not very real to her yet. He was a kind of miracle that she had seen happen and that she talked about but that she still didn't believe."[16] Her euphoria is cut short, however, when she learns that he has been accepting money from one of her black hired hands. The money is part of a plan to bring his sixteen-year old cousin from a Polish work camp to this country. In exchange, he promises the girl's hand to the black man. Mrs. McIntyre is appalled and disillusioned. She stumbles upon truth in her conclusion that "they're all the same," but she does not yet see that she is herself of that sameness. She decides to announce to the priest that she will let the Guizacs go at the end of the month, but in their conversation, she and the priest talk at cross purposes. In the process she reveals her unconsciously formulated complaints to God.

> He sat on her porch, taking no notice of her partly mocking, partly outraged expression as she sat shaking her foot, waiting for an opportunity to drive a wedge into his talk. "For," he was saying, as if he spoke of something that had happened yesterday in town, "when God sent his Only Begotten Son, Jesus Christ Our Lord"—he slightly bowed his head—"as a Redeemer to mankind, He . . ."
>
> "Father Flynn!" she said in a voice that made him jump. "I want to talk to you about something serious!"
>
> The skin under the old man's right eye flinched.
>
> "As far as I'm concerned," she said and glared at him fiercely, "Christ was just another D.P."[17]

In a striking piece of O'Connor irony, Mrs. McIntyre has spoken the truth. Her intention of course was to scandalize, but she has stumbled upon a truth so profound that the priest cannot respond to it. Because the Incarnation was the most spectacular displacement in history, Christ was a displaced person in the deepest sense of that phrase. He began His earthly life displaced into a stable, rejected by the people of His home town, and He was finally displaced from this life by the crucifixion. Mrs. McIntyre has seen the truth, but it has not made her free. She dreams that the priest is speaking to her of the Holocaust: "Dear lady, I know your tender heart won't suffer you to turn the porrrr man out. Think of the thousands of them, think of the ovens and the boxcars and the camps and the sick children and Christ Our Lord." Mrs. McIntyre answers in her dream, "He's extra and he's upset the balance around here."[18] Unwittingly, in her attitude toward Mr. Guizac, she reveals her attitude toward Christ. He is extra and He has upset the balance. In an earlier conversation, while the priest had been describing the Transfiguration, her thoughts had been preoccupied with Guizac. "Christ will come like that!" the priest had said, pointing to the peacock. "He didn't have to come in the first place," Mrs. McIntyre responds several lines later, referring to Guizac. The priest, who is still thinking of the peacock and not really concentrating on Mrs. McIntyre's words, replies, "He came to redeem us."[19]

These conversations work like emblems. The emblem, as an unusual literalization of a scriptural truth, relies on exaggeration and pun, as well as on strange, unsettling juxtapositions. While the conversation between the priest and Mrs. McIntyre is not a visual enactment of a spiritual truth in the same sense that an emblem might be, it does capture the spirit of the emblem in its paradoxical, even ambiguous use of language. In a real sense, Mr. Guizac does come to serve as an agent in the redemption of Mrs. McIntyre, although it is Christ who is actually the Redeemer. With the Guizacs comes the priest, who until the end of her life will never stop explicating church dogma to Mrs. McIntyre. But even more important, with Mr. Guizac's death, Mrs. McIntyre is forced to confront her own capacity for sin and evil—something one feels she has never done before—and which is an absolutely essential step toward her salvation. When Mr. Guizac is crushed by the tractor, she, Mr. Shortley, and the Negro are passive spectators, paralyzed by the cold, perhaps, but all, in reality, guilty of murder.

She heard the brake on the large tractor slip and, looking up, she saw it move forward, calculating its own path. Later she remembered that she had seen the Negro jump silently out of the way as if a spring in the earth had released him and that she had seen Mr. Shortley turn his head with incredible slowness and stare silently over his shoulder and that she had started to shout to the Displaced Person but that she had not. She had felt her eyes and Mr. Shortley's eyes and the Negro's eyes come together in one look that froze them in collusion forever, and she had heard the little noise the Pole made as the tractor wheel broke his backbone.[20]

Here is an emblem in which greed and ignorance crush another human being, in the process transforming Mrs. McIntyre into a displaced person. Watching the priest administer the sacrament of last rites, "she felt she was in some foreign country where the people bent over the body were natives, and she watched like a stranger while the dead man was carried away in the ambulance."[21] Up to this point her life has been lived apart from sacrament, and apart from a real sense of responsibility for others, even though she has often spoken of the extra responsibilities she has had to assume.

Finally, she loses most of her land, she loses her health, she loses feeling in one of her legs, she loses control of her muscles, she loses her eyesight, but she has learned the meaning of displacement. She has been forced to confront herself as a fallen, sinful human being and this has changed her life forever. The final emblem of the story shows the priest arriving with his bag of breadcrumbs for the peacocks, feeding them, and then sitting by Mrs. McIntyre's bedside, expounding the doctrines of the Church, feeding her bit by bit, week after week—breaking the bread of life. This is sacrament, the outward and visible sign of an inner and spiritual truth. For Mrs. McIntyre, whose senses are almost entirely dead, sacrament, which connects the sensory being with the eternal, seems impossibly distant.

In a book in O'Connor's personal library appears the following explanation of sacrament: " . . . a sacrament is no mere sign, no mere figure for a known reality which exists in our experience quite apart from its sign. A 'known reality' is, in this sense, something remembered, a fact or an idea, which, because of its complexity, is conveniently indicated by a sign of greater simplicity. Thus a sacrament is not an allegorical action, a way of representing something which the participants 'understand' in some other and more direct manner. The 'material part' of a sacrament, the 'matter' which it employs and the 'form' in which it is employed, always signifies what is otherwise *unknown*. That is to say, it signifies the real and present world which cannot be remembered and is never, therefore, an object of knowledge."[22] Sacrament, then, connects the known with the unknown.

In other stories the physical, outer reality—sometimes in grotesque forms—creates a graphic emblem of spiritual truth. Revelation in "A Temple of the Holy Ghost" occurs in a circus tent, in a dream, and in the sacrament of the Eucharist. The recipient of the sacred insight is a twelve-year-old girl. The title refers to a verse from 1 Corinthians 6 (RSV): "Do you not know that your body is a temple of the Holy Spirit within you, which you have from God? You are not your own; you were bought with a price, so glorify God in your body." This emphasis on the physical pervades the entire story. Unappealing physicality is emphasized from the first sentence: "All weekend the two girls were calling each other Temple One and Temple Two, shaking with laughter and getting so red and hot that they were positively ugly, particularly Joanne who had spots on her face anyway."[23] The circus tent freak is in many ways no more repulsive physically to the child than Alonzo Myers, the smelly, sweaty taxi driver who drives the visiting cousins from the convent to the child's house, and back again. In addition, Mr. Cheatam, Miss Kirby's suitor, "was bald-headed except for a little fringe of rust-colored hair and his face was nearly the same color as the unpaved roads and washed like them with ruts and gulleys."[24] The country boys who accompany the cousins to the fair are "short thin boys with red faces and high cheekbones and pale seed-like eyes."[25] For the child the physical is often an insurmountable reality, but at the same time, it is still in part a mystery. Neither she nor her cousins, for example, know how rabbits are born, even though she says that she has seen a mother rabbit spit the babies out of her mouth.

The visiting cousins know the verse from Corinthians because they have been warned by Sister Perpetua to guard themselves, to keep their physical natures holy, particularly if they ever find themselves in the back seat of a car with a young man. The sexual knowledge of these girls is sparse; they seem to know only a little more than the child herself, but all three recognize something strange in the nun's admonitions. The cousins' reaction is hysterical laughter, but knowing that she is the temple of the Holy Ghost makes the child "feel as if someone had given her a present."[26] She understands right away the universal application of her newly discovered knowledge and immediately concludes that even Miss Kirby is a temple of the Holy Ghost.

In the New Testament, the Holy Spirit is the giver of gifts, one of which is prophecy, such as Mrs. Shortley experienced in "The Displaced Person." The Holy Spirit, as the giver of life, is also considered the purveyor of freedom from a slavish entanglement with the law. O'Connor's story is grounded in the understanding that the gospel is the ultimate fulfillment of the law and the final freedom from the law's condemnation.[27] Another passage from 1 Corinthians refers to the body as the temple of the Holy Spirit and then proceeds to define wisdom, using Old Testament writings.

Do you not know that you are God's temple and that God's spirit dwells in you? If any one destroys God's temple, God

"It breaks my heart to leave for a whole summer."

Cartoon originally published in "Colonnade," volume XIX, no. 18, p. 2, May 30, 1944, Georgia College, Milledgeville, Georgia.

will destroy him, for God's temple is holy, and that temple you are. Let no one deceive himself. If any one among you thinks that he is wise in this age, let him become a fool that he may become wise. For the wisdom of this world is folly with God. For it is written, "He catches the wise in their craftiness" and again "The Lord knows that the thoughts of the wise are futile" (1 Corinthians 3, RSV).

So it is not that the law is dead in O'Connor's works; it is, rather, that the law sometimes functions to lead the characters to the conviction of their sins, and, thus, indirectly to the gospel message that their sins are forgiven in Christ. In the meantime, as Paul indicates, the world is turned upside down. Wisdom is folly. Foolishness is wise. Early in "A Temple of the Holy Ghost" the mother admonishes the child, who is giggling hysterically over her own suggestion that Mr. Cheatam might show her cousins around. "Her mother told her if she didn't stop this foolishness she would have to leave the table."[28] It is the child's foolishness and the freak's that will finally lead her to truth (with the help, of course, of the Holy Spirit).

The Holy Spirit also finds its place in the fiercely trinitarian "Tantum Ergo . . ." that the cousins sing for the country boys. This hymn is about the old law giving way to the new dispensation. It is about the Father and the Son and it is about the Holy Spirit, who proceeds from the Father and the Son. It is, in short, the gospel message. Significantly, the boys do not understand it because the girls sing it in Latin. One boy calls it "Jew singing" and, of course, completely misses the point. The cousins who sing it are actually no more enlightened than the boys, but the child, hiding in the bushes, cannot contain herself as she yells at the one boy, "You big dumb Church of God ox!"

For the child, although she may not consciously realize it yet, the entire world is filled with God's grace. The fairground, secularistic, dirty, and lewd, seems an unlikely forum for God's word, but the fair's beacon light seems to search the heavens for "the lost sun." Here O'Connor's pun illuminates again. The fallen world needs the Son to save it from everlasting night. The light revolves "up and around and away,"[29] in circular motions just as the child imagines the "diamond ring of the ferris wheel going around and around up in the air and down again and the screeking merry-go-round going around and around on the ground."[30] These circles are movements that reflect the eternal. The child also imagines the circus tents, spectacularly painted with figures like "martyrs waiting to have their tongues cut out by the Roman soldiers." The fair, which local preachers will force to close is, ironically, fraught with God's presence.

The child imagines herself as a martyr in something like a circus tent, thereby connecting herself with the freak she will dream about later. She is primed, ready for the Spirit to descend and to impart understanding. She even explains herself using religious paradox: "She would have to be a saint . . . yet she knew she would never be a saint."[31] She is all too aware of her propensity to sin, an important first step in the direction of redemption.

The child, in her ability to use the physical in reaching the spiritual, shows her strong sacramental training and it is because of this training that she is able to use the freak as a vehicle to arrive at a more profound understanding of the incarnation. The freak's androgyny is a peculiarly effective emblem of Christ's dual nature—divinity and humanity in one person. The child wonders how the freak can be both male and female and not have two heads. But further than this—the child understands that the freak is actually more than just a combination of two physical natures. The freak is also a temple of the Holy Ghost and in the child's dream, the freak creates a liturgy in which all of the spectators find a part, too.

She lay in bed trying to picture the tent with the freak walking from side to side but she was too sleepy to figure it out. She was better able to see the faces of the country people watching, the men more solemn than they were in church, and the women stern and polite, with painted-looking eyes, standing as if they were waiting for the first note of the piano to begin the hymn. She could hear the freak saying, "God made me thisaway and I don't dispute hit," and the people saying, "Amen, Amen."

"God done this to me and I praise Him."

"Amen. Amen."

"He could strike you thisaway."

"Amen. Amen."

"But he has not."

"Amen."

"Raise yourself up. A temple of the Holy Ghost. You! You are God's temple, don't you know? Don't you know? God's Spirit has a dwelling in you, don't you know?"

"Amen. Amen."

"If anybody desecrates the temple of God, God will bring him to ruin and if you laugh, He may strike you thisaway. A temple of God is a holy thing.

"Amen. Amen."

"I am a temple of the Holy Ghost."

"Amen."

The people began to slap their hands without making a loud noise and with a regular beat between the Amens, more and more softly, as if they knew there was a child near, half asleep.[32]

This dream-liturgy combines Roman rite, Bible-church rhythms and sideshow spectacle. In it is the truth of the redemption—a redemption which extends even to our corrupt physical natures.

To reinforce the connection, the freak reappears in the middle of the mass at the end of the story. The child, now kneeling and

hearing the "Tantum Ergo," begins her mechanical prayers:
" 'Hep me not to be so mean . . . . Hep me not to give her so
much sass. Hep me not to talk like I do.' Her mind began to get
quiet and then empty but when the priest raised the monstrance
with the Host shining ivory-colored in the center of it, she was
thinking of the tent at the fair that had the freak in it."[33] Earlier
the child had tried to look at the ivory sun directly, but had to
filter its light through her hair. The divine is too bright to face
head-on, but when she uses a part of her body as a type of lens,
she can discern with greater clarity. Here in the mass and the
sacrament of the Eucharist she finds the connection between
ivory sun and ivory wafer, between sun and Son, between the
freak and Jesus, between herself and God.

Significantly, her senses are open and fed by this experience.
This is not a merely ethereal epiphany. It involves her whole
physical being. She has just ridden in the taxi with smelly Alonzo,
who "they had thought . . . would smell better on Sunday but
he did not." Now in the chapel she smells incense. She hears
the "Tantum Ergo." As she leaves, the nun hugs her, emblematically "mashing the side of her face into the crucifix hitched onto
her belt."[34] On the way home in Alonzo's taxi, the child notices
Alonzo's folds of fat and pig ears. But she is more distant now.
She is thinking.

> Her mother let the conversation drop and the child's round
> face was lost in thought. She turned it toward the window
> and looked out over a stretch of pasture land that rose and
> fell with a gathering greenness until it touched the dark
> woods. The sun was a huge red ball like an elevated Host
> drenched in blood and when it sank out of sight, it left a line
> in the sky like a red clay road hanging over the trees.[35]

Recall Mrs. Shortley's "gaze down the red clay road," and Mr.
Cheatam's face, "the same color as the unpaved roads." Clay is

the material of human existence, what we are made of and what
the child has in front of her now—a red clay road, mundane,
probably rutted, but redeemed, just as the circus freak, deformed
as he is, is a temple of the Holy Ghost.

The Holy Ghost, the Lord and Giver of life, also figures prominently in "The Enduring Chill." Asbury returns home from New
York where he had moved to become a writer. Suffering from
fever and chills, certain that he is dying, he allows his mother
to put him to bed, but he refuses to see a doctor. The doctor
comes anyway and eventually diagnoses Asbury's illness as un-
dulant fever, contracted from drinking unpasteurized milk.

Shortly after picking him up from the train station, his mother
had stopped the car to look at one of her sick cows. Asbury
turned his head away, "but there a small, walleyed Guernsey
was watching him steadily as if she sensed some bond between
them. 'Good God!' he cried in an agonized voice, 'can't we go
on? It's six o'clock in the morning!' "[36] Once again, as in so many
of O'Connor's stories, taking God's name in vain adds a strongly
ironical tone. God is in that cow and in Asbury's illness which
came from cow's milk, and it is through this infection from cow's
milk that God will finally be able to reach Asbury. In his delirium
he sees a herd of cows "and one large white one, violently spot-
ted . . . softly licking his head as if it were a block of salt."[37] His
doctor's name, not too coincidentally, is Dr. Block. The illness
contracted from cows, and the doctor's tests and his diagnosis
of the illness will combine to push Asbury closer to revelation.

The story works emblematically in other ways, too. The keys
to Asbury's drawer (in which he keeps the long letter meant to
be read by his mother when he dies) are mentioned often enough
that they draw particular attention to themselves. Keys in Scripture and iconography are associated with St. Peter, and this story
provides echoes and emblematic interpretations of several passages from the first two chapters of 1 Peter. Peter refers to the
spiritual milk which new Christians require: "As newborn babes,

"Coming Back Affects Some People Worse Than Others."

Cartoon originally published in "Colonnade," volume XVII, no. 22, p. 2, March 20, 1943, Georgia College, Milledgeville, Georgia.

desire the sincere milk of the word, that ye may grow thereby:
If so be ye have tasted that the Lord is gracious" (2:2-4). Significantly, Asbury does not like milk, but the last time he had been
home he had drunk the tainted raw milk out of the Negroes'
glass, in a vain effort to entice them to drink with him from a
common cup. They would not drink because Asbury's mother
had forbidden them ever to drink raw milk. For Asbury the
danger of raw milk is not the issue at all; he is more interested
in defying the segregational taboos of his culture and irritating
his mother. The Negroes simply do not want to violate one of
the laws of proper dairying, especially after their last "communion," smoking in the barn with Asbury, had resulted in tainted
milk.

Asbury's dreams contain other details reminiscent of images
from 1 Peter, where Christ is described as "a living stone" and
his followers as "lively stones" (1 Peter 2:4-5). Asbury dreams of
"two large boulders . . . circling each other inside his head."[38]
The Jesuit priest who, much to the mother's dismay, answers
Asbury's summons, is a surprise and disappointment to Asbury,
who had expected someone with whom he could converse about
James Joyce and the myth of the dying god. Instead, the priest
gets right down to the most important business of all.

> "What do you think of Joyce?" Asbury said. . . .
> "Joyce? Joyce who?" asked the priest.
> "James Joyce," Asbury said and laughed.
> The priest brushed his huge hand in the air as if he were
> bothered by gnats. "I haven't met him," he said. "Now. Do
> you say your morning and night prayers?"
> Asbury appeared confused. "Joyce was a great writer," he
> murmured, forgetting to shout.
> "You don't, eh?" said the priest. "Well, you will never learn
> to be good unless you pray regularly. You cannot love Jesus
> unless you speak to Him."

"The myth of the dying god has always fascinated me," Asbury shouted, but the priest did not appear to catch it.

"Do you have trouble with purity?" he demanded, and as Asbury paled, he went on without waiting for an answer. "We all do but you must pray to the Holy Ghost for it. Mind, heart and body. . . ."

". . . Who made you?" the priest asked in a martial tone.

"Different people believe different things about that," Asbury said.

"God made you," the priest said shortly. "Who is God?"

"God is an idea created by man," Asbury said, feeling that he was getting into stride, that two could play at this.

"God is a spirit infinitely perfect," the priest said. "You are a very ignorant boy."[39]

The priest continues to quiz Asbury on the catechism he does not know and finally says to him, "The Holy Ghost will not come until you see yourself as you are—a lazy ignorant conceited youth!" He berates the mother for neglecting her spiritual duties to her son and concludes by repeating, "He's a good lad at heart but very ignorant."[40] Peter's call in the first chapter of 1 Peter is to be "obedient children, not fashioning yourselves according to the former lusts in your ignorance" (v. 14).

O'Connor plays with many traditional symbols and images of the Holy Ghost in this story. Most often illustrated as a dove, the Holy Spirit is linked thematically with the Jesuit priest at the meeting Asbury attends in New York. The priest's name, Ignatius Vogle, suggests both his Jesuit roots (Ignatius Loyola) and a connection with the Holy Spirit (vogel is the German word for bird). In addition, the priest refers directly to the Holy Ghost when questioned by Asbury. "There is," the priest said, "a real probability of the New Man, assisted, of course . . . by the Third Person of the Trinity."[41] He hands Asbury a card, but Asbury never calls on him. God has already started his work, however, and Asbury becomes even more ill.

Asbury complains of being a martyr to art, of being handed the desire to create, but not the talent. His writing is lifeless and his imagination is dead. As the Lord and Giver of life, the Holy Spirit in Asbury's life has been almost entirely excluded, so it is no wonder that his artistic spirit should be frozen, too. In fact, the dove he imagines in the cracks of his bedroom ceiling is really dripping icicles. He has always felt that the dove was about to descend and set an icicle on his head. His chills worsen. After the blind priest's admonition that God will not send the Holy Spirit to anyone who does not ask for it, Asbury notices the bird more frequently and feels "it was there for some purpose that he could not divine."[42]

When he discovers that he is not dying, but is ill with a disease that will come and go throughout his life, the "blinding red-gold sun" begins to penetrate the wall he has set up against it.

> The old life in him was exhausted. He awaited the coming of new. It was then that he felt the beginning of a chill, a chill so peculiar, so light, that it was like a warm ripple across a deeper sea of cold. His breath came short. The fierce bird which through the years of his childhood and the days of his illness had been poised over his head, waiting mysteriously, appeared all at once to be in motion. Asbury blanched and the last film of illusion was torn as if by a whirlwind from his eyes. He saw that for the rest of his days, frail, racked, but enduring, he would live in the face of a purifying terror. A feeble cry, a last impossible protest escaped him. But the Holy Ghost, emblazoned in ice instead of fire, continued, implacable, to descend.[43]

The disease, the chill, is the vehicle for the Holy Spirit. It is an illness which brings revelation. It is an illness which will never leave him. Here the flames of fire (for Asbury the flames of fever) associated with Pentecost and the coming of the Holy Spirit to the disciples are encased, impossibly, paradoxically, in ice. For Asbury it is only his enduring chills, the persistent reminders that death, the final chill, is a breath away—it is only this ice in the midst of his life fever that will finally allow him to receive revelation and cast away his illusions. This is no abstract and ineffectual "communion" in the barn, nor does it provide intellectual titillation for him. Instead, it is an experience felt with the senses, and in that sense is naturally sacramental. The new life he awaits will come with the Spirit's descent. For Asbury the kingdom of God is at hand.

In "The River" O'Connor works directly with the sacrament of baptism—a theme to which she will return later in her novel, *The Violent Bear It Away*. In the story O'Connor develops a "two kingdoms" theology which explores the ramifications and ambiguities of the Christian life, anchored on earth, but focused on heaven. She establishes a contrast between the worldly life and the spiritual life, creating an intricate series of associations. Harry Ashfield's parents, for example, neglect the basic needs of their child because their lives are so consumed with drinking, partying, and recovering from hangovers. His mother paints her toenails red, and wears "long black satin britches," traditional garb of the worldly woman. She does no nurturing, and after his baptism Harry feels that her questions are attempts to pull him out of the river, which he now associates with the kingdom of God.

Likewise, at the end of the story Mr. Paradise, the sinister figure who sits beyond the crowd of believers and taunts them, makes a futile attempt to rescue Harry from the river. He has gone after the child to entice him with a candy cane, "nourishment" similar to that Harry has received at home. Do Mr. Paradise's evil intentions (he has chased the child) give way as

he tries to rescue the drowning child? Or is Mr. Paradise attempting to save him so he can play out his evil purposes? The question
is left unanswered, although the final description leaves little
doubt that Mr. Paradise is not a true savior figure: "The old man
rose like some ancient water monster and stood empty-handed,
staring with his dull eyes as far down the river line as he could
see."[44]

Mr. Paradise's ear is covered with a purple cancer, a detail
which connects him with Mrs. Connin's hog which was "long-leg-
ged and humpbacked and part of one of his ears had been bitten
off."[45] The hog, a traditional symbol of sensuality and gluttony,
also finds thematic development in the picture book Mrs. Connin
reads to Harry—"The Life of Jesus Christ for Readers Under
Twelve." The child has never before heard of Jesus, and having
just a few minutes before escaped from the hog which was chasing him (as Mr. Paradise will later chase him), he listens with
particular interest to the story of "the carpenter driving a crowd
of pigs out of a man."

In the one kingdom—the earthly life of Harry Ashfield—the
hog, Mr. Paradise, and his parents predominate. In the other
kingdom is Mrs. Connin who feeds Harry breakfast and reads
him the gospel, and Jesus, who banishes the hogs. But Mrs.
Connin, although she is a caretaker and provides for Harry's
needs as she is able, lives with several dull and apparently evil
children. One feels the particular dilemma of a two kingdoms'
theology in her life. She is hardworking—a good woman—but
her physical life is unattractively anchored in paucity. Her spirit
may be alive—she is committed to truth—but she has no real
sense of transcendence. When the preacher begins to speak about
the kingdom of God, therefore, associating it with baptism in
the river, it becomes an attractive alternative to the child. He
disassociates himself physically from his parents, and does not
consider Mrs. Connin's home a safe haven, so it is only appropri-

ate that he actually be re-christened Bevel, becoming in a sense the spiritual son of the preacher whose name is also Bevel. At home, among the unredeemed he is Harry. Baptized in the river, he is Bevel.

Notice how even though O'Connor has established the dichotomy between those who know the *spiritual* value of the gospel and those who understand that the Bible story book Harry steals is *monetarily* valuable, the categories of sacred and profane are not absolute. As in "Parker's Back" where swearing becomes almost indistinguishable from praying, "The River" opens with Mrs. Connin complaining that the child is not ready to leave the house because "he ain't fixed right." "Well then for Christ's sake fix him," the father says. It will be precisely for Christ's sake that Mrs. Connin will have Harry baptized. Later, the child thinks: "They joked a lot where he lived. If he had thought about it before, he would have thought Jesus Christ was a word like 'oh' or 'damn' or 'God,' or maybe somebody who had cheated them out of something sometime."[46]

David Jones has pointed out that "there is a time-honoured distinction between the 'sacred' and the 'profane'. It is a distinction valid enough and useful enough in certain contexts—just as is the distinction between 'religious' and 'secular.' But properly speaking and at the root of the matter, [Art] knows only a 'sacred' activity." He compares the word *sacred* with the word *sacrament*, concluding that both words need "to be rescued from certain antipathetic biases."[47] That is exactly what O'Connor is doing here. The profane and the sacred come so close to one another that at times they become almost indistinguishable, a phenomenon closely related to the emblem O'Connor presents in the final scene (and later picks up even more graphically in the drowning-baptism at the end of *The Violent Bear it Away*), where the child drowns in the same water in which he was baptized. One is reminded of T. S. Eliot's "Journey of the Magi" and the question the magus asks.

. . . were we led all that way for
Birth or Death? There was a Birth, certainly,
We had evidence and no doubt. I had seen birth and death
But had thought they were different; this Birth was
Hard and bitter agony for us, like Death, our death.[48]

This is the doubleness of paradox. On the one hand the preacher
at the riverside says, "If you ain't come for Jesus, you ain't come
for me. If you just come to see can you leave your pain in the
river, you ain't come for Jesus. You can't leave your pain in the
river." On the other hand he says, "There ain't but one river and
that's the River of Life, made out of Jesus' Blood. That's the river
you have to lay your pain in."[49] These two rivers—one with a
small "r" and the other with a capital "r"—are indistinguishable
to the common observer. Certainly the child does not distinguish
between them.

> "If I Baptize you," the preacher said, "you'll be able to go
> to the Kingdom of Christ. You'll be washed in the river of
> suffering, son, and you'll go by the deep river of life. Do you
> want that?"
> "Yes," the child said, and thought, I won't go back to the
> apartment then, I'll go under the river.[50]

It is in this strange experience that Roman Catholic sacrament
and fundamentalist practice come together. In a review of Gus-
tave Weigel's *Faith and Understanding in America* O'Connor describes Weigel's conclusions and provides her own commentary
on them.

> He points out that Catholics, while neither fundamentalists
> nor liberals are doctrinally closer to Protestant fundamentals
> than to those liberal Protestant theologians who have created
> a naturalistic ethical culture, humanism, and labeled it Chris-

tianity. This, although Father Weigel does not mention it, is
of particular interest to the Catholic in the South. . . . It is an
embarrassment to our fundamentalist neighbors to realize that
they are doctrinally nearer their traditional enemy, the Church
of Rome, than they are to modern Protestantism.[51]

Recall how careful the preacher is to make the distinction between
the efficacy of river water in healing, and the use of the water
in the act of baptism. Almost Lutheran in his understanding of
baptism as the combination of Word and Sacrament, he says,
"This old red river is good to Baptize in, good to lay your faith
in, good to lay your pain in, but it ain't this muddy water here
that saves you."[52] Whether or not he realizes it, however, he is
presenting sacrament—the outward and visible sign of an inner
and spiritual grace—in its most profound form. Unavoidably
sacramental, O'Connor sees the catholicity of the fundamentalist
baptism. Whether or not the preacher realizes it, he is a sacramentalist.

In describing the fiction writer, O'Connor also describes the
preacher: "The real novelist, the one with an instinct for what
he is about, knows that he cannot approach the infinite directly,
that he must penetrate the natural human world as it is."[53] This
natural human world contains common natural phenomena infused with the grace of God—the water in the river, and the sun
(the Son) following at a distance "as if it meant to overtake
them."[54] The oddness of O'Connor's vision lies in the doubleness
associated with the theology of the two kingdoms, and her sacramental orientation which allows everything in this world to
be both sacred and profane.

O'Connor realized that she was speaking to a world which
did not recognize the spiritual realm at all. In her well-known
comments in which she refers obliquely to this story and more
overtly to *The Violent Bear It Away*, she says:

When I write a novel in which the central action is a baptism, I am very well aware that for a majority of my readers, baptism is a meaningless rite, and so in my novel I have to see that this baptism carries enough awe and mystery to jar the reader into some kind of emotional recognition of its significance. To this end I have to bend the whole novel—its language, its structure, its action. I have to make the reader feel, in his bones if nowhere else, that something is going on here that counts.[55]

That is Harry-Bevel's phrase. He "counts" now, he tells his mother.

Three years after this story was published, O'Connor was approached by a man who wanted to make a film of it. She wrote to "A" that "he has never made a movie before but is convinced 'The River' is the dish for him—'a kind of documentary,' he said over the telephone. It is sort of disconcerting to think of somebody getting hold of your story and doing something else to it and I doubt if I will be able to see my way through him. But we shall see. How to document the sacrament of Baptism???????"[56] She was wary because she knew that the sacraments are visible, but work invisibly. They connect the two kingdoms and both participate in and resolve the paradoxes of the faith.

— 5 —

And the Blind Shall See

In all of O'Connor's stories and most dramatically in the stories covered in this chapter, the gospel fights its way through against all odds. Blindness is stripped away and because the characters would often rather not see at all than see the truth about themselves, the process is excruciating. A similar phenomenon occurs in the reader. Christian readers, for example, thrown off balance by O'Connor's violence, the ugly characters, the odd references to Christ, often find themselves curiously put on the defensive about the relative strength of their own faith. Non-Christians are often O'Connor fans without knowing precisely why. Often these are readers who stumble unwittingly on the truths O'Connor is shoving at them.[1]

Some fine writers and scholars have revealed much about their faith backgrounds in the comments they have made about O'Connor. One of the most surprising is Eudora Welty who said, "Flannery O'Connor I only got to meet, I am sorry to say, towards the end of her life, when we both worked at giving college readings, and we corresponded some. I was crazy about her, and I wish I could have known her better. It took me a while to realize the things I didn't know about her work, the spiritual force of them. I wasn't acquainted with the Roman Catholic Church and concepts like grace, I had to find out. Of course I loved her stories on any level."[2] This is one of the South's leading writers confessing that before reading O'Connor she was not acquainted with the concept of grace, the very basis of Christianity. Her comment is simultaneously a strong indicator of O'Connor's influence and a frightening indictment of Western culture, which seems to be losing the myths which created it. O'Connor's task was to reinstate these myths, to revitalize them, to take a religious language permeated with clichés and show that underneath the inadequate expression was a truth worth restating.

The first story readers confront is usually "A Good Man Is Hard to Find," probably the most frequently anthologized of all of O'Connor's stories. Many students complain about the extremes to which O'Connor pushes her characters in this story. An entire family—a mother, father, three children, including an infant, and a grandmother—are shot by an escaped convict, who calls himself The Misfit. The ending surprises and disappoints students, but when they return to the story, they discover that the violent ending of this story is inevitable from the very first paragraph.

The family is driving to Florida, but the grandmother would rather go to Tennessee. She tries to change her son's mind and says, "Here this fellow that calls himself The Misfit is aloose from the Federal Pen and headed toward Florida and you read here what it says he did to these people. Just you read it. I wouldn't take my children in any direction with a criminal like that aloose in it. I couldn't answer to my conscience if I did."[3] Ironically, the grandmother will ultimately be the one responsible for taking the family in the direction of The Misfit.

References to death permeate the story. The grandmother does not want to leave her cat alone at home because "he might brush against one of the gas burners and accidentally asphyxiate himself."[4] She dresses as if she were going to church so that "in case

"The whole family's been wintering here at GSCW [Georgia State College for Women]—you have to take what you can get these days."

Cartoon originally published in "Colonnade," volume XIX, no. 15, p. 2, May 2, 1944, Georgia College, Milledgeville, Georgia.

of an accident, anyone seeing her dead on the highway would know at once that she was a lady."[5] The car passes a family graveyard that is an island in the middle of a cotton field. The grandmother refers to Mr. Teagarden, her former suitor, who is now dead and then she naps until they pass through *Tooms*boro. The family stops at The Tower for lunch. The references accumulate until there is no longer any doubt that death is imminent— that death, in fact, is the story.

In "A Late Encounter with the Enemy," written a year or two earlier than "A Good Man Is Hard to Find," O'Connor had described a one-hundred-and-four-year-old Confederate soldier who does not concern himself with seeing clearly. Although his memory is non-existent, and his senses are almost dead, he is taken out now and then for display purposes. For him, and for his sixty-two-year-old granddaughter, being seen is what is important. At the end of the story, the "general" finally recovers snatches of memory in the seconds before his death. His past is revealed to him, stabs of pain awaken him, and he then sits staring fiercely with his eyes wide open, seeing nothing because he is dead. Revelation comes to him only when he encounters death. This revelation is not spiritual, however, but historical, even though O'Connor uses the sun (one of her most familiar symbols of Christ's presence) as an agent of death.[6]

For the grandmother in "A Good Man Is Hard to Find," death is also a necessary companion to revelation. It is only when she realizes that she is going to die that she is able to look beyond herself to another human being and recognize the interconnectedness of all humanity. Her son, Bailey, is shot in the woods and stripped of his shirt, which The Misfit puts on. The old lady, hysterical with terror, talks nonstop to The Misfit, telling him that he is really a good man, that he should pray to Jesus.

"Jesus!" the old lady cried. "You've got good blood! I know you wouldn't shoot a lady. I'll give you all the money I've got!"

"Lady," The Misfit said, looking beyond her far into the woods, "there never was a body that give the undertaker a tip. . . ."

"Jesus was the only One that ever raised the dead." The Misfit continued, "and He shouldn't have done it. He thrown everything off balance. If He did what He said, then it's nothing for you to do but throw away everything and follow Him, and if He didn't, then it's nothing for you to do but enjoy the few minutes you got left the best way you can—by killing somebody or burning down his house or doing some other meanness to him. No pleasure but meanness," he said and his voice had become almost a snarl.[7]

Death is necessary for resurrection to occur and it is resurrection which The Misfit discusses with the old lady before he shoots her. She says, "Maybe He didn't raise the dead." He responds, "I wasn't there so I can't say He didn't. . . . Listen lady . . . if I had of been there I would of known and I wouldn't be like I am now." At this point the old lady responds to the poignancy of The Misfit's dilemma. He has suffered for no reason he can surmise. He is angry and wants to make his crimes fit the punishments he has already received. He is uncertain, but he wants to believe.[8] Furthermore, he is now wearing Bailey's shirt. So she reaches out to him, she responds to him as if he were her own child, she shows the stirrings of compassion, seeing him as a fellow sufferer, and he shoots her immediately.

The struggle between the grandmother and the criminal is primarily verbal. She, with her unwitting prayers (so close to swearing) and her frantic flattery, has reminded him of his major spiritual problem. He, in turn, has unintentionally provided a strange but powerful Christian witness for the grandmother, who "would of been a good woman . . . if it had been somebody there to shoot her every minute of her life."[9]

This story provided O'Connor with humorous and exasperat-

ing subject matter for the rest of her life. In comments preceding
a reading of this story, O'Connor explained some of her frustra-
tions with outrageous interpretations of it.

> I've talked to a number of teachers who use this story in class
> and who tell their students that the Grandmother is evil, that
> in fact, she's a witch, even down to the cat. One of these
> teachers told me that his students, and particularly his South-
> ern students, resisted this interpretation with a certain be-
> mused vigor, and he didn't understand why. I had to tell him
> that they resisted it because they all had grandmothers or
> great-aunts just like her at home, and they knew, from per-
> sonal experience, that the old lady lacked comprehension, but
> that she had a good heart. The Southerner is usually tolerant
> of those weaknesses that proceed from innocence, and he
> knows that a taste for self-preservation can be readily com-
> bined with the missionary spirit.
>   This same teacher was telling his students that morally the
> Misfit was several cuts above the Grandmother. He had a
> really sentimental attachment to the Misfit. But then a prophet
> gone wrong is almost always more interesting than your grand-
> mother, and you have to let people take their pleasures where
> they find them.
>   It is true that the old lady is a hypocritical old soul; her wits
> are no match for the Misfit's, nor is her capacity for grace
> equal to his; yet I think the unprejudiced reader will feel that
> the Grandmother has a special kind of triumph in this story
> which instinctively we do not allow to someone altogether
> bad.[10]

The emblem in this story is the grandmother's final gesture, in
which she reaches for The Misfit and he recoils "as if a snake
had bitten him" and then shoots her three times. O'Connor says
"the grandmother's head cleared for an instant" before she

reached for him. She finally sees clearly. But it is the terror of death, and the recognition of her own mortality that has brought her to this point. Death is a powerful instructor.

Sightedness is also a major theme in "A View of the Woods," which introduces the vision motif in its title. Flannery O'Connor called this story "a little morality play" and in a letter to "A," referred to the woods as "the Christ symbol."[11] The view of the woods, then, becomes the position from which one sees the incarnation. For Mary Fortune, the view is clear. When her grandfather decides to sell the field in front of the house, she is upset because she will no longer be able to see the woods. The grandfather does not understand. In one of O'Connor's typically subtle uses of irony, she has the grandfather say, "There's not a thing over there but the woods."[12] He retreats to his room to rest, but cannot keep himself from going to the window now and then to look at the line of trees. "A pine trunk is a pine trunk, he said to himself, and anybody that wants to see one don't have to go far in this neighborhood."[13]

One does not need O'Connor's explanation of the story to see the connection between the woods and the mystery of the incarnation. In the first paragraph the "woods appear at both ends of the view to walk across the water,"[14] mimicking both Christ's action and Peter's. Later the child stares at the line of woods "as if it were a person that she preferred to [her grandfather]."[15] Then comes the emblematic moment in the story, when the grandfather is afforded a glimpse of the glory of God, even though he does not really understand it.

> The third time he got up to look at the woods, it was almost six o'clock and the gaunt trunks appeared to be raised in a pool of red light that gushed from the almost hidden sun setting behind them. The old man stared for some time, as if for a prolonged instant he were caught up out of the rattle of everything that led to the future and were held there in the

midst of an uncomfortable mystery that he had not apprehended before. He saw it, in his hallucination, as if someone were wounded behind the woods and the trees were
bathed in blood. After a few minutes this unpleasant vision
was broken by the presence of Pitts's pick-up truck grinding
to a halt below the window. He returned to his bed and shut
his eyes and against the closed lids hellish red trunks rose up
in a black wood.[16]

At the hour of compline, time is momentarily suspended. The
old man sees the sunset, so often used by O'Connor to refer to
Christ, behind the trees. He sees the blood of suffering, and the
passion. He sees the prophecy of his own death in the woods,
and he attempts to shut out the vision because it shows him
something he cannot tolerate.

He bases his life, instead, on a different emblem. He stands
for progress—and it is progress that will take away the view of
the woods. It is progress that allows the bulldozer in to eat the
clay of his land, clay which so often in scripture refers to the
stuff of life which God shapes to form humankind. O'Connor
seems to be playing here with many scriptural echoes, but one
particular passage is remarkable for its parallels with this story.

Isaiah 29 is in part a prophecy of the woe Israel will experience
because of its blindness and its refusal to heed God's warnings:
"For the LORD hath poured out upon you the spirit of deep
sleep, and hath closed your eyes: the prophets and your rulers,
the seers hath he covered. And the vision of all is become unto
you as the words of a book that is sealed, which men deliver to
one that is learned, saying, Read this, I pray thee: and he saith,
I cannot; for it is sealed . . ." (vv. 10-11). Mr. Fortune cannot
read the signs of the Lord. He is discomfited by them, and he
squeezes his eyes to close them out.

Isaiah continues to develop the image of God as potter, responding with rhetorical questions to those (the potter's clay)

who would hide from him: ". . . for shall the work say of him that made it, He made me not? or shall the thing framed say of him that framed it, He had no understanding?" (v. 16). The presence of clay opens and closes "A View of the Woods," in both cases in the jaws of the huge steam-shovel clearing Mr. Fortune's land. References to the red, corrugated lake and the red earth pervade the story. God's cry from Jeremiah—"Behold, as the clay is in the potter's hand, so are ye in mine hand, O house of Israel"—has a particular resonance in this context. Mr. Fortune will not listen to the warning. He actually edges as close as he can to the pit the bulldozer is digging—and he encourages Mary Fortune to do the same. Here is another emblem—the bottomless pit from Scripture—the pit from which the psalmist has been saved: "He brought me up also out of a horrible pit, out of the miry clay, and set my feet upon a rock, and established my goings" (Psalm 40:2).

After he signs away the land, and Mary Fortune has tried to hit him with a bottle, he experiences a terrible sense of urgency and anger. "His heart felt as if it were the size of the car and was racing forward, carrying him to some inevitable destination faster than he had ever been carried before."[17] He goes to the woods with the child, prepared to beat her for the first time in his life, but after removing her glasses, she fights him viciously, knocking his glasses off, too, taunting him with her victory over him. In one violent surge of energy he rolls her over and brings her head down on a rock, a grotesque reversal of the position of the psalmist's feet in Psalm 40, above. She is dead, her eyes "rolled back down and were wet in a fixed glare that did not take him in." [18] And then without his glasses (reminiscent of The Misfit's final gesture) he begins to see as he has never seen before. He falls back and the woods seem to converge on him. He looks for an escape route as he imagines himself being drawn faster and faster toward the water. "He realized suddenly that he could not swim and that he had not bought the boat. On both sides of him he saw that the gaunt trees had thickened into mysterious dark files that were marching across the water and away into the distance."[19] He is dying and in his last few seconds he is being forced to walk upon the water even though, like Peter, he will need Christ's help.

Earlier in the story is another hint that O'Connor is thinking of Peter. She describes the old man's relationship with his granddaughter: "He had frequent little verbal tilts with her but this was a sport like putting a mirror up in front of a rooster and watching him fight his reflection."[20] The rooster is the traditional symbol of Peter's denial of Christ and his eventual awakening and repentance.

The awakening comes late in the story, and also late in Isaiah 29, but it is there. In Isaiah the redemption of Israel is described metaphorically as a desert becoming a fruitful field and the fruitful field "esteemed as a forest" (v. 17). This is a reversal of Mr. Fortune's intentions of making the field into a wasteland which would block out the view of the forest. Isaiah continues to develop the motif of sightedness: "And in that day shall the deaf hear the words of the book, and the eyes of the blind shall see out of obscurity and out of darkness" (v. 18). Five times in the final paragraph of the story O'Connor uses verbs of sight and seeing to refer to the old man. He has already looked "behind him for a long time at the little motionless figure with its head on the rock."[21] He sees the child he has killed. Isaiah 29 ends: "But when he seeth his children, the work of mine hands, in the midst of him, they shall sanctify my name, and sanctify the Holy One of Jacob, and shall fear the God of Israel. They also that erred in spirit shall come to understanding, and they that murmured shall learn doctrine." On the surface the story seems bleak. But beyond the cruelty, selfishness and hatred of these characters is the possibility of their redemption. And in O'Connor's stories, God breaks through somewhere and somehow.

A line of trees also figures significantly in "A Circle in the

Fire." Mrs. Cope is obsessed with the fear that fire will destroy "her" woods. Only her fat, twelve-year-old child sees the connection between the fear of fire and the sun, another of O'Connor's references to the Son of God. Here the two symbols unite to suggest God's doubly irresistible grace.

> The child thought the blank sky looked as if it were pushing against the fortress wall, trying to break through. The trees across the near field were a patchwork of gray and yellow greens. Mrs. Cope was always worrying about fires in her woods. When the nights were very windy, she would say to the child, "Oh, Lord, do pray there won't be any fires, it's so windy. . . ." Mrs. Cope would say to the child who was reading fast to catch the last light, "Get up and look at the sunset, it's gorgeous. You ought to get up and look at it," and the child would scowl and not answer or glare up once across the lawn and two front pastures to the gray-blue sentinel line of trees and then begin to read again with no change of expression, sometimes muttering for meanness, "It looks like a fire. You better get up and smell around and see if the woods ain't on fire."[22]

Mrs. Cope, one of O'Connor's classically blind characters, hears and reads of the suffering of other people (the Negroes, the "Europeans ridden in boxcars like cattle"), but she is too self-absorbed to feel anything but gratefulness that she has been spared suffering. In fact, even death is only a vague reality to her. When the three city boys speak to her for the first time, she asks Powell about his father, who had worked for her some years before. Powell reports that his father is dead. " 'Dead. Well I declare,' Mrs. Cope said as if death were always an unusual thing. 'What was Mr. Boyd's trouble?' "[23]

The child is curious about these boys, who are strange, double figures in this tale. They are part devil, creating mischief and havoc wherever they are let loose, letting the bull out of the pen, throwing rocks at the mailbox, bathing in the cow trough, riding the forbidden horses, letting oil out of the tractors. But these boys are also attracted irresistibly to Mrs. Cope's farm, which, of course, contains the trees and the peculiar sunset. One of the boys reports that Powell said once that "when he died he wanted to come here!"[24] The boys see the truth which Mrs. Cope cannot see. They see that even though the forest is part of her farm, she finally does not own the trees. Mrs. Pritchard, the hired help, reports a conversation between the boys and her husband.

> "This morning Hollis seen them behind the bull pen and that big one ast if it wasn't some place they could wash at and Hollis said no it wasn't and that you didn't want no boys dropping cigarette butts in your woods and he said, 'She don't own them woods,' and Hollis said, Shes does too,' and that there little one he said 'Man, Gawd owns them woods and her too,' and that there one with the glasses said, 'I reckon she owns the sky over this place too,' and that there littlest one says, 'Owns the sky and can't no airplane go over here without she says so.' "[25]

Just as the symbol of fire can refer both to the destructive judgment of God and the vital fires of Pentecost, bringing the gifts of the Comforter, so also do these boys possess a doubleness of identity, emblematized by Powell's eyes, one of which "had a slight cast to it so that his gaze seemed to be coming from two directions at once as if it had them surrounded."[26] His eyes also constantly make "a circle of the place."[27] O'Connor has used circles before to refer to the eternal, often brooding presence of God. It should come as no surprise, then, that these boys, in their mischief—and even in their final destructive act—become the agents of God, who has been trying for some time, it seems, to break through to Mrs. Cope.

The emblematic moments in this story provide the allegorical impetus. The boys come toting a "black pig-shaped valise," which, Mrs. Pritchard discovers, is filled with food. They do not eat Mrs. Cope's food (and it is to her credit that she does try to feed them), but they do drink milk from the barn and ask her for water. She sees hunger on their faces, and against her better judgment she allows them to spend one night in the field, thus responding inadvertently to Christ's direction to feed the hungry, satisfy the thirsty, and take in the stranger. She, of course, cannot give them the type of food or shelter they require. They must steal the milk from her, and she is helpless to force them off her land. She cannot respond to their needs, because she has not recognized that she, too, is needy.

The story opens with Mrs. Pritchard's description of a woman who had a baby thirteen months after she began treatment in an iron lung—a fact that arouses Mrs. Pritchard's curiosity and her judgment about what is and what is not proper behavior for a woman in an iron lung. Mrs. Cope hardly seems to be listening, but the image becomes her own emblem. She, too, has a child whom she ignores and fails to nourish. She does not hear other people and when she speaks, she communicates in comfortable abstractions and clichés. She does not feel. She merely exists, no more alive than that woman in an iron lung, whose breathing has to be done by a machine. What a contrast to the three boys who finish their romp in the cow trough with a race around the field, and then lie on the ground "with their ribs moving up and down."[28]

When the boys set her woods on fire, the mother appears as she has never been seen before. Her child looks at her, shocked into a new awareness. "It was the face of the new misery she felt, but on her mother it looked old and it looked as if it might have belonged to anybody, a Negro or a European or to Powell himself."[29] As she watches her woods burn, she realizes her link with others who have suffered in the past. She becomes one of those she pitied earlier in the story.

And the prophets who have brought her this news? The boys

"dancing in the fiery furnace, in the circle the angel had cleared for them." These are Shadrach, Meshach and Abednigo from Daniel 4—thrown by King Nebuchadnezzar into the fiery furnace, and preserved by the Lord to be a witness to the King.[30]

O'Connor also seems to be playing with Christ's parable of the wheat and the tares (Matthew 13:24-30, 37-43). Like the story, the parable displays a quality of doubleness. A man sowed good seed in his field, but while he slept, his enemy sprinkled his field with weeds. When the servants of the farmer noticed the weeds growing among the wheat, they asked their master what they should do, and he advised them to let both weeds and wheat grow together until the harvest, at which time the weeds could be gathered separately and burned.

Mrs. Cope seems to spend all her time pulling weeds. In fact, "she worked at the weeds and nut grass as if they were an evil sent directly by the devil to destroy the place."[31] She can never stay ahead of the weeds, however, and she expresses her frustration, but also her pride, in her life of endless work, which she insists has made her what she is. Mrs. Pritchard, on the other hand, although she is always present while Mrs. Cope is working, never works much herself. She expresses what seems to be her life philosophy in her attitude toward the three boys. "There ain't a thing you can do about it," she advises Mrs. Cope. "What I expect is you'll have them for a week or so until school begins. They just figure to have themselves a vacation in the country and there ain't nothing you can do but fold your hands."[32] But Mrs. Cope is unaccustomed to remaining idle. She will not stay still long enough to receive the free gift of grace, so it must come and seize her most violently.

All of the significant images in "A Circle in the Fire" are also found in Christ's explanation of the parable of the wheat and the tares. The field, the devil, the angels, the weeds, the children, the fire of judgment, the shining sun, and the fiery furnace combine in both story and parable to show how fire can become the instrument of revelation. What will be left after the fire will be a bleak landscape, but in the story Mrs. Cope's blindness shall have been stripped away.

A similar bleakness pervades "Everything That Rises Must Converge." O'Connor said in a letter to Roslyn Barnes that she took the title from a concept she discovered in Pierre Teilhard de Chardin's writing.[33] We know that she reviewed *The Phenomenon of Man* in 1960 and *The Divine Milieu* early in 1961, about the time she was finishing "Everything That Rises . . . ." In one of these reviews O'Connor says that "it is doubtful if any Christian of this century can be fully aware of his religion until he has reseen it in the cosmic light which Teilhard has cast upon it."[34] That she uses the verb of seeing and the image of light is particularly appropriate, for Teilhard entitled his foreword to *The Phenomenon of Man*, "Seeing." He felt that all of life was in the verb "to see," that "to see is really to become more."[35] He wrote, "I doubt whether there is a more decisive moment for a thinking being than when the scales fall from his eyes and he discovers that he is not an isolated unit lost in the cosmic solitudes, and realises that a universal will to live *converges* and is hominised in him" (italics mine).[36] The converging process is painful but inevitable in O'Connor's story, and the title of the story introduces the concept immediately. But first must come the rising.

Before the end of the story, Julian's mother will have suffered a stroke—an event foreshadowed in the story's first sentence. "Her doctor had told Julian's mother that she must lose twenty pounds on account of her blood pressure, so on Wednesday nights Julian had to take her downtown on the bus for a reducing class at the Y. The reducing class was designed for working girls over fifty, who weighed from 165 to 200 pounds."[37] Her blood pressure has risen because her weight has risen. In response to his mother's explanation about her new hat, "Julian raised his eyes to heaven." Later, the mother will say about blacks: "They should rise, yes, but on their own side of the fence."[38] Later, after she has been hit by the black woman, Julian notices that "rising above them on either side were black apartment buildings, marked with irregular rectangles of light."[39] More than mere curious coincidences, these elements—the weight, the blood pressure, Julian's eyes, the blacks, the buildings—represent the forces which must converge to correct Julian's vision.

Julian is one of O'Connor's "ignorant" intellectuals. He has an education, but he, like Hulga-Joy in "Good Country People" cannot support himself. He still lives at home with his mother and he thinks of himself as a martyr, sacrificed, he believes, to her pleasure.[40] His is a martyrdom without spiritual content. At one point he is described as "saturated in depression, as if in the midst of his martyrdom he had lost his faith."[41] He is arrogant and hateful, planning petty ways to get back at his mother for what he perceives as her prejudice against blacks, but in the process he reveals his own.

Many students of O'Connor mistakenly identify Julian's motives as admirable, a conclusion so remarkable yet so prevalent that one begins to believe that this is the result of an intentional ploy on O'Connor's part. She wants readers to identify with Julian, to feel frustration with his mother, to experience his blindness as their own so that they can also feel the final convergence, the ultimate stripping away and the violent revelation at the end. Often readers' sympathies are so entirely with Julian that they do not see his intellectual arrogance and his savagery. But, of course, if they do not see his problem, the ending of the story makes no sense at all—for it is only after he realizes that his mother is dying that he sees their relationship—and himself—clearly for the first time. Even though Julian is completely dependent on his mother, he does not recognize himself as such. He thinks he has separated his identity from hers.

Similarly, his mother feels an arrogant superiority toward the black race. She buys a purple and green hat and is sure she "won't meet herself coming and going," but that is precisely

"I think it's perfectly idiotic of the Navy not to let you WAVES dress sensibly like us college girls."

Cartoon originally published in "Colonnade," volume XVIII, no. 25, p. 2, April 10, 1943, Georgia College, Milledgeville, Georgia.

what she must do in this story. The emblematic moment occurs when a black woman, wearing the same hat, boards the bus Julian and his mother are riding. Julian is amused, and as the woman sits down next to him and the black woman's child sits next to his mother, he hopes his mother sees the irony involved in this confusion of mothers and sons. Julian himself does not yet see the real importance of this scene—that all of humankind is linked—and that we all meet ourselves coming and going.

In a chapter on "The Personalising Universe" from *The Phenomenon of Man* Teilhard de Chardin confronts this issue.

In trying to separate itself as much as possible from others, the element individualises itself . . . . In fact it diminishes itself and loses itself. To be fully ourselves it is in the opposite direction, in the direction of convergence with all the rest, that we must advance—towards the 'other.' The peak of ourselves, the acme of our originality, is not our individuality but our person; and according to the evolutionary structure of the world, we can only find our person by uniting together. There is no mind without synthesis.[42]

Until the final paragraphs Julian cannot separate his mind from the mind of his mother or the mind of the world. But then he realizes that there is something terribly wrong with her, that she is probably dying and he cries out to her, for the first time naming her "mother." She falls and he cries, "Mamma, Mamma!" He rushes forward to get help but "the tide of darkness seemed to sweep him back to her, postponing from moment to moment, his entry into the world of guilt and sorrow."[43] The convergence has occurred.[44]

O'Connor said of this story that she'd "like to write a whole bunch of stories like that, but once you've said it, you've said it."[45] She was probably referring to Teilhard's theory of convergence, because in actuality, the themes of blindness and of sight, of sudden revelation and of violent death permeate her work. In two of her stories, "Greenleaf" and "Revelation," these themes find their most overt expression.

"Greenleaf" introduces Mrs. May who is pursued by God from the first sentence of the story to the last, when he finally captures her in a deadly embrace. The informing emblems occur in two scenes—the first and the last. To begin with, "Mrs. May's bedroom window was low and faced on the east and the bull, silvered in the moonlight, stood under it, his head raised as if he listened—like some patient god come down to woo her—for a stir inside the room."[46] The east is traditionally associated with the second coming of Christ, so Mrs. May, although she does not believe that the name of Jesus should be used outside of church, is, as she sleeps, in the proper position to be awakened by Christ when he arrives. Significantly, the bull *has* arrived outside her window "like some patient god." He is crowned with a wreath, and he has been lost for a resonant three days.

Importantly, Mrs. May views this bull only as a threat. He has come, she believes, to ruin her herd—and in this creature, a scrub-bull, she finds a connection with the Greenleafs who own him. They are "scrub-humans," she says, when one of her sons teases her with the threat of marrying a woman like Mrs. Greenleaf someday. Her sons, she is afraid, will one day "marry trash and ruin everything."[47]

Frederick Asals has pointed out the scriptural echoes in this story. To begin with he cites the Song of Songs, which presents a type of Christ wooing his Church: "My beloved is like a roe or a young hart: behold, he standeth behind our wall, he looketh forth at the windows, showing himself through the lattice."[48] The connections with the first paragraph of the story seem intentional. Asals also identifies Jeremiah 17:8 as providing a possible source both for Mrs. Greenleaf's name and her prolificacy, and also a humorous connection with her primitive religious activity. ("For he shall be as a tree planted by the waters, and that spreadeth out her roots by the river, and shall not see when heat cometh, but her leaf shall be green; and shall not be careful in the year of drought, neither shall cease from yielding fruit.") When Mrs. May hears Mrs. Greenleaf moaning, "Jesus, Jesus," Mrs. May feels as if "some violent unleashed force had broken out of the ground and was charging toward her,"[49] an ironic prophecy of her own death (and another overt connection between Jesus and the bull), but she is also repulsed and embarrassed by "Mrs. Greenleaf sprawled obscenely on the ground."[50] Here is another example of O'Connor's juxtaposition of the sacred and the profane.

Mr. Greenleaf, Mrs. May's hired man and her antagonist for fifteen years, "walked on the perimeter of some invisible circle,"[51] another of O'Connor's familiar symbols of the eternal. That the circle is invisible ties in with the important theme of sight and blindness in this story. Mrs. May cannot see reality, even though she yells at her sons, "You'll find out one of these days, you'll find out what *Reality* is when it's too late."[52] The fact is that she cannot bear very much reality and that is why she tries to keep Mrs. Greenleaf out of her sight. She also cannot admit that the Greenleaf boys have done better than she has, and when she steps into their milking barn, she is momentarily dazzled by its blinding whiteness. Furthermore, at one point in the story her vision is blurred by tears and when her vision clears she goes to the window to observe the "black wall of trees with a sharp sawtooth edge." We've seen these trees before in other stories, and O'Connor always identifies them with Christ. Here the sawtooth edge both reminds one of the crown of thorns the bull's wreath echoed, and prefigures the violence Mrs. May will have to encounter as she is brought into sightedness. At this point she sees, but she doesn't understand.

In the final scene of the story, the sun beats through her closed eyes.

> With her eyes closed, she didn't think of time as divided into days and nights but into past and future. She decided she was tired because she had been working continuously for fifteen years. She decided she had every right to be tired, and to rest for a few minutes before she began working again. Before any kind of judgement seat, she would be able to say: I've worked, I have not wallowed.[53]

Like Mrs. Cope in "A Circle in the Fire," and Mrs. McIntyre in "The Displaced Person," Mrs. May considers work her salvation. There is no room for faith or grace.

> At this very instant while she was recalling a lifetime of work, Mr. Greenleaf was loitering in the woods and Mrs. Greenleaf was probably flat on the ground, asleep over her holeful of clippings. The woman had got worse over the years and Mrs. May believed that now she was actually demented. "I'm afraid your wife has let religion warp her," she said once tactfully to Mr. Greenleaf. "Everything in moderation, you know."[54]

She is still, seconds before her death, a skeptic, and even when she opens her eyes to see the bull racing joyously toward her, she stares in "freezing unbelief."[55] But as his horn pierces her heart, her blindness is torn away. "She continued to stare straight ahead but the entire scene in front of her had changed—the tree line was a dark wound in a world that was nothing but sky—and she had the look of a person whose sight has been suddenly restored but who finds the light unbearable."[56]

This final violent emblem is of Christ claiming His own. Mrs. May has finally understood the wretched fact of her own mortality—but the only way this truth could pierce her was in confronting death, not as abstraction, but as a specific and personal event. God has pushed her to the brink, and she has had to go over the edge before she could receive revelation.

For Mrs. Turpin in the story "Revelation," O'Connor prescribes less drastic measures. The story opens in a doctor's waiting room with a gospel hymn playing faintly in the background—a hymn to which Mrs. Turpin mentally supplies the words. She knows the forms of religion, she would probably talk freely about her personal relationship with Jesus, but she does not realize that she shares with the rest of Christendom a double identity—as both saint and sinner. Mrs. Turpin is most comfortable with clear definitions, with distinct, unambiguous categories. She tries to avoid thinking about people who do not fit neatly into her pre-conceived system of social hierarchy.

Sometimes Mrs. Turpin occupied herself at night naming the classes of people. On the bottom of the heap were most colored people, not the kind she would have been if she had been one, but most of them; then next to them—not above, just away from—were the white-trash; then above them were the home-owners, and above them the home-and-land owners, to which she and Claud belonged. Above she and Claud were people with a lot of money and much bigger houses and much more land. But here the complexity of it would begin to bear in on her, for some of the people with a lot of money were common and ought to be below she and Claud and some of the people who had good blood had lost their money and had to rent and then there were colored people who owned their homes and land as well. There was a colored dentist in town who had two red Lincolns and a swimming pool and a farm with registered white-face cattle on it. Usually by the time she had fallen asleep all the classes of people were moiling and roiling around in her head, and she would dream they were all crammed in together in a box car, being ridden off to be put in a gas oven.[57]

The emblematic moment in this story occurs as Mrs. Turpin sits in the waiting room, praying self-righteous prayers of thanksgiving to Jesus for giving her such a good disposition. Abruptly, Mary Grace, a college student whose well-dressed mother has been speaking with Mrs. Turpin, throws a book (titled *Human Development)* at Mrs. Turpin, and then attempts to strangle her. In the middle of her "Thank you, Jesus, Jesus, thank you," the book hits Mrs. Turpin above her left eye. God's intervention could not be more clear. While Mary Grace is being restrained and sedated, Mrs. Turpin leans over the girl and asks her what she has to say, "waiting, as for a revelation."[58] Mary Grace answers, "Go back to hell where you came from, you old wart hog."

Mrs. Turpin interprets this as a message from God and she is hurt and puzzled by it. "The message," she complains, "had been given to Ruby Turpin, a respectable, hard-working, church-going woman."[59] It is significant that in the waiting room the one woman who expresses open prejudice and is overtly unpleasant and even insulting is *not* the object of Mary Grace's anger. Instead, it is Mrs. Turpin, who masks her prejudices with smiles and waves, who feels she is a good person. That she is hit over her eye is significant, for she must be given new vision.

Mrs. Turpin returns home and tells her Negroes about what has happened to her, but she is not satisfied with their response. They flatter her, telling her she is pretty and that Jesus is satisfied with her. "Idiots," she says to herself.

As she hoses off the hogs, she begins to see the truth—in another emblematic scene. The hogs, traditional symbols of evil and gluttony, must be cleaned every day. It is their nature to be dirty, and Mrs. Turpin takes great pride in her clean "pig parlor."

"Targets are where you find 'em!"

Cartoon originally published in "Colonnade," volume XVIII, no. 23, p. 2, March 27, 1943, Georgia College, Milledgeville, Georgia.

But as she stands hosing them down, she begins to see connections—between the hogs and herself. The sun goes down behind the trees and reminds her of "a farmer inspecting his own hogs"[60]—and there she is straddling two kingdoms. Christ the Sun is the farmer watching her, His "hog," while she, the farmer, stands watching her own hogs. She is both redeemed, identified with Christ himself, and sinner, identified with the "wart hogs from hell."

"Who do you think you are?" she yells to God, and he answers with an echo of her very words. She has nothing more to say, so she watches Claud's truck disappear down the highway and she recognizes, probably for the first time, just how vulnerable he is—and she is; that an accident could at any minute "scatter Claud's and the niggers' brains all over the road."[61]

As the sun sets she is afforded a vision which corrects her perception. She sees a bridge from heaven to earth and a procession of white-trash, Negroes, lunatics, and bringing up the rear, people like herself and her husband. "She could see by their shocked and altered faces that even their virtues were being burned away." The sun falls behind the trees, and she makes her way home in the dark, seeing and hearing clearly for the first time.

In "Revelation," as in the other stories covered in this chapter, the scales crusting the characters' eyes must be violently torn away. In only this one story, written in the last months of O'Connor's life, does the character survive the painful procedure. One critic has complained that "the concept of God suggested by her work is in the last resort hardly more reassuring than her Devil," and that she "is definitely on the darker fringe of Christianity."[62] O'Connor is, one must remember, speaking to the post-holocaust age. That she was critically aware of the concentration camps is evident in the many references throughout her stories to the European boxcars crowded with people being carted to the gas chambers. It is a picture that appears often enough to be consid-

"She says we're on the threshold of social revolution."

Cartoon originally published in "Colonnade," volume XX, no. 10, p. 4, April 5, 1945, Georgia College, Milledgeville, Georgia.

ered an informing metaphor, if not an emblem, of modern civilization. Having confronted absolute evil, many Christians consider "the darker fringe" the only tenable spot to hang one's faith—that is, the darkest fringe, the cross, where God the Son experienced the silence of God the Father. Flannery O'Connor never leaves us in the ambiguity of silence, however. In her stories the blind finally do see, spectacularly.

6

One Step Forward and Two Back:
Wise Blood

Wise Blood, *O'Connor's first novel, is about a modern pilgrim* who does not want to progress, who is in fact more interested in moving backwards than forwards. In her note to the second edition, O'Connor calls Hazel Motes a Christian *malgré lui* in a "comic novel," which is "very serious"[1] (the connections with Dante's *The Divine Comedy* are made clear from the beginning). Other critics have noticed the mythic, almost typological qualities in Hazel Motes' journey. Martha Stephens has called the novel a "bitterly serious, if sometimes outlandishly comic, version of the Christian travail."[2] Frederick Asals has labeled the novel a "modern pilgrim's progress of a blaspheming believer,"[3] and Miles Orvell has noted the similarity to Bunyan's methodology in the novel's pattern. The novel is not, Orvell suggests, allegorical in the traditional sense, "for it attempts to render an image of experience that is more complex than that of the traditional allegory and that cannot be so easily translated, at every point, into its theological or dogmatic equivalent."[4] The allegory O'Connor is working with is closely tied to emblem, just as *The Pilgrim's Progress* had its strongly evocative, emblematic roots.[5] The mythic journeys of both Christian in the seventeenth-century work and

Hazel Motes in the twentieth-century novel trace emblematic routes through death to salvation. The difference is that Christian holds on to the ideal of salvation, and this surety allows him to persevere, even though he succumbs to temptation and experiences backsliding along the way. Hazel, on the other hand, has ostensibly rejected the ideal, and he attempts over and over again to regress, to deny God, to reject salvation.

Hazel Motes is a man on the run. From the beginning of the novel to the end he is constantly in motion, whether on a train, in a car, or on foot in his final death walk. Like O. E. Parker who joined the navy to avoid God, Hazel is running from Jesus, who is chasing him, who is moving "from tree to tree in the back of his mind, a wild ragged figure motioning him to turn around and come off into the dark where he was not sure of his footing, where he might be walking on the water and not know it and then suddenly know it and drown."[6] As one of O'Connor's reluctant prophets, Hazel has from childhood been aware that for some reason God has chosen him. His grandfather prophesied that Jesus "would chase him over the waters of sin."[7] In return, Hazel vowed that he would avoid sin and thereby avoid having to confront Jesus.

No matter how circuitous Hazel's route, he cannot avoid the presence of God. Even though O'Connor does not develop her sun, sky and tree line symbols in this novel as she does in her later stories, one still feels the omnipresence of an invisible but powerful force behind Hazel.[8] This force occasionally is objectified in symbol: the "large blinding white [cloud] with curls and a beard" which directs Hazel's journey down a clay road[9]; the "I see you," with which Sabbath Lily taunts him as she stands behind a tree (similar to the tree Jesus hides behind in the back of Hazel's mind); the sun which appears in the second sentence of the novel, "standing, very red, on the edge of the farthest woods."[10]

It is because Hazel feels this presence that he runs so fast and

with such ingenuity. This running is emphasized by all the references to feet in the novel. As a child, Hazel puts stones in his
shoes and waits for a sign from God (a sign which never comes),
prefiguring his final weeks of life when he again fills his shoes
with stones. This penitential act keeps him from running as fast.
The rocks and pebbles slow his pace enough that God will be
able to catch him. Between these two incidents, one early and
one late in his life, are two other references to feet. In an attempt
to seduce Hazel, Sabbath Lily pulls open her collar and lies on
the ground, saying, "Ain't my feet white, though?"[11] Later, before
Hazel gives in to her, he sits looking at his feet—"big and white
and damp."[12] Here the feet are connected with sexual sin—yet
another version of stones in the shoes. Just as the stones will
allow God to capture Hazel, so the sin of fornication will force
Hazel to acknowledge the presence of God. He has known since
childhood and his grandfather's prophecy that sin and the need
for Jesus are intimately connected.

Before Hazel meets Sabbath Lily, he decides that he wants to
avoid sin and preach the gospel (a strange combination, for without sin there is no need for the gospel). His gospel, however, is
different, he says, because he preaches "the church of truth
without Jesus Christ Crucified."[13] He abruptly begins his ministry on the train. "I reckon you think you been redeemed," he
says to the lady facing him, and later to the women in the dining
car. He means to tell them they have not, but he never gets
beyond saying that he wouldn't believe in Jesus "even if He
existed. Even if He was on this train."[14] They are insulted and
uncomfortable with such direct talk. Hazel, who is running from
God, is much more comfortable talking about Him than they are.

Hazel's grandfather had been similarly on the move. As a
circuit preacher he "had ridden over three counties with Jesus
hidden in his head like a stinger."[15] For him redemption and
movement had been as connected as they will be for Hazel.
Significantly, when Hazel reaches Taulkinham, he will buy a car.

In an exchange which shifts from the profane to the sacred, Hazel bargains for the old "rat-colored" automobile in the used car lot.

> Haze moved quickly from the far side of the car and came around in front. "How much is it?" he asked.
>
> "Jesus on the cross," the boy said, "Christ nailed."
>
> "How much is it?" Haze growled, paling a little.
>
> "How much do you think it's worth?" the boy said. "Give us a estimit."
>
> "It ain't worth what it would take to cart it off. I wouldn't have it."[16]

The fact is that the car will cost Hazel his unbelief. The price will truly be Jesus on the cross. The cursing boy fills his tank before he drives the car and murmurs, "Sweet Jesus, sweet Jesus, sweet Jesus."[17] In purchasing the car, Hazel hopes to run from Jesus more effectively, but he will discover that because of the car he will be forced to confront Jesus more squarely. At one point he yells, "Nobody with a good car needs to be justified."[18] The loss of the car after its use as an instrument of murder will force him back to his feet and prove to him just how much he does need to be justified in the eyes of God.

While Hazel is being chased, he is also doing some chasing himself. He is attracted irresistibly to the blind Asa Hawks and his daughter Sabbath, who preach on street corners and hand out tracts. Although Hazel denies his faith and attempts to dissuade passers-by from their Christian beliefs, he cannot hide his Christian calling even from these strangers. Asa knows it at once. "I can hear the urge for Jesus in his voice," he says.[19] Even the taxi-driver who drives Hazel from the train station to the home of Leora Watts ("the friendliest bed in town")[20] recognizes Hazel as a preacher. When Haze says to Leora Watts, "What I mean to have you know is: I'm no goddam preacher," she responds, tickling his chin, "That's okay, son . . . . Momma don't mind if you ain't a preacher."[21] Enoch Emery also tells Haze that "I knew when I first seen you you didn't have nobody nor nothing but Jesus."[22] Near the end of the book the landlady correctly concludes that "you must believe in Jesus or you wouldn't do these foolish things."[23]

His foolishness has been that he has moved around a lot, but he hasn't really gone anywhere. In his attempt to escape Jesus, he has not put any distance at all between them. Frederick Asals concludes that "Haze's desperate unacknowledged search for Jesus . . . gives his paradoxical journey meaning only on the spiritual level, for the forward physical movement takes him, in every sense, nowhere."[24] After he blinds himself, he finally looks as if he is moving forward toward something he can see. Ironically, for the first time he is perfectly still.

> His face had a peculiar pushing look, as if it were going forward after something it could just distinguish in the distance. Even when he was sitting motionless in a chair, his face had the look of straining toward something.[25]

At the end of the novel he is blind, but he sees; he is motionless, but he moves; he is sinner and he is redeemed.

This contradiction with its roots in the two-kingdoms' theology, which views humankind as both tied to the earth and straining toward heaven, informs all of Hazel's actions in the book. Near the beginning he insists, "I am clean. If Jesus existed, I wouldn't be clean."[26] At the end of the book he insists, "I'm not clean."[27] This is a novel about his conversion from one statement about his soul to the other, but the transition is not neat. There is doubt in each statement—some of the truth of each contention resides in the other.

Though at first he says he does not believe in sin, he shows a remarkable understanding of original sin. "If I was in sin I was in it before I committed any. There's no change come in me . . . I don't believe in sin."[28] His last statement is qualified by the doubts expressed in his knowledge about original sin. He is contradicting himself and revealing his rootedness in scriptural truth, while at the same time denying it. In this respect he is very much like the man who says to Jesus, "Lord, I believe; help thou mine unbelief" (Mark 9:24). O'Connor quoted this passage in one of her letters when she wrote to a friend, "I don't know how the kind of faith required of a Christian living in the 20th century can be at all if it is not grounded on this experience that you are having right now of unbelief . . . . Peter (sic) said, 'Lord, I believe. Help my unbelief.' It is the most natural and most human and most agonizing prayer in the gospels, and I think it is the foundation prayer of faith."[29]

From the first sentence of the novel the picture the reader has of Hazel Motes is that of a man who is not settled, who does not have a clear direction.

> Hazel Motes sat at a forward angle on the green plush train seat, looking one minute at the window as if he might want to jump out of it, and the next down the aisle at the other end of the car.[30]

His physical appearance and choice of clothing also give contradictory signals: "He didn't look . . . much over twenty, but he had a stiff black broad-brimmed hat on his lap, a hat that an elderly country preacher would wear."[31] As he walks down the street in Taulkinham, his shadow occasionally makes him appear to be heading two directions at once:

> Haze's shadow was now behind him and now before him and now and then broken up by other people's shadows, but when it was by itself, stretching behind him, it was a thin nervous shadow walking backwards. His neck was thrust forward as

if he were trying to smell something that was always being drawn away.[32]

He finds himself watching Asa Hawks, not knowing whether to leave him or to follow him. "He stood staring after him, jerking his hands in and out of his pockets as if he were trying to move forward and backward at the same time."[33]

This approach-avoidance motion is echoed in passages in which the sacred and the profane become almost indistinguishable. "Jesus . . . my Jesus," Haze mutters after the blind man has heard "the urge for Jesus" in Hazel's voice.[34] Sabbath Lily calls this cursing, but as with Ruller in "The Turkey," or Parker in "Parker's Back," or so many other characters in O'Connor's stories, cursing and prayer move felicitously close to one another.

One critic has also noticed that Hazel begins to reveal his contradictory nature early during his army years. When he is asked to accompany his friends to a brothel, his voice cracks, revealing his real desires. M. Bruce Gentry observes, "It occurred not because he really wanted to go to a brothel, but because he feared that if he succeeded in returning uncorrupted to Eastrod and staying there, he might succeed in avoiding Jesus. It is typical of Hazel that a movement into wordlessness should say more about his unconscious desires than his conscious statements do."[35] Hazel says one thing and believes another.

This duplicity reveals itself in a conversation he has with Sabbath Lily. She announces that she is a bastard and asks if a bastard can be saved in his church.

"There's no such thing as a bastard in the Church Without Christ," he said. "Everything is all one. A bastard wouldn't be any different from anybody else."

"That's good," she said.

He looked at her irritably, for something in his mind was already contradicting him and saying that a bastard couldn't, that there was only one truth—that Jesus was a liar—and that her case was hopeless. . . . The thing in his mind said that the truth didn't contradict itself and that a bastard couldn't be saved in the Church Without Christ.[36]

In one of his sermons he preaches that what people need is his Church Without Christ, and what his church needs is a new jesus—one that is all man, but one "that don't look like any other man so you'll look at him."[37] The androgynous freak in "Temple of the Holy Ghost" was just such a man—and people did look at him, but the point of that story was that because the freak was like no other man, he was able to embody the truth of Christ, who was also like no other man. Haze says he will set this new jesus up and "then you'll know once and for all that you haven't been redeemed. Give me this new jesus, some-body, so we'll all be saved by the sight of him."[38] Again Haze contradicts himself. "There's no peace for the redeemed," he says. "Look at me . . . and you look at a peaceful man. . . ."[39] He considers himself a peaceful, unredeemed man, but he is preaching redemption by the sight of the new jesus.

When Enoch Emery takes Hazel to the museum to see the new jesus, a mummified, shrunken man in a glass case, Hazel looks into the glass and sees a reflection of himself and a woman standing nearby. He makes a noise which "might have come from the man inside the case. In a second Enoch knew it had."[40] Hazel makes the sounds of the new jesus and the emblem is complete. In the center of the tabernacle—the museum of natural history—filled with stuffed birds (false replicas of the Holy Spirit), Hazel views his new creation—the jesus which his church has lacked. He is actually the father of this jesus—a god attempt-ing to create a new mythos, but not really wanting any converts.

Significantly, later in the novel, after Enoch steals the new jesus from the glass case in the museum and leaves it with Sabbath, she cradles it as if it were a baby. In a strange parody

of the Nativity scene, she becomes the new jesus' mother and
runs to show the "baby" to Haze. "Call me Momma now," she
says to Haze. Looking at the baby, she asks, "Ask your daddy
yonder where he was running off to. . . . Ask him isn't he going
to take you and me with him?"[41] Haze picks up the jesus and
flings him against the wall, breaking his head off, and then
throws him out the door into the pit.

Marion Montgomery has noted the similarity in tone and in
metaphorical complexity between this "creche-scene" and many
of the poems of John Donne, known for his metaphysical wit
and his ability to yoke disparates together by violence.[42] Writing
in the seventeenth century with the emblem-book tradition as
a persistent influence,[43] Donne wrote poems whose strange effects are similar in many ways to O'Connor's. His odd combina-
tions of sex and religion, similar to the experiences of the mystics
(in particular St. Teresa of Avila and Saint John of the Cross) find
curious echoes in O'Connor's fiction. Here in Haze's bedroom
we hear those echoes as Haze insists that he is now leaving for
another city in order to preach the truth of The Church Without
Christ.

> "And when were you going?" she asked.
> "After I get some more sleep," he said, and pulled off the
> glasses and threw them out the door.
> "You ain't going to get none," she said.[44]

When Haze finally gains a "convert," the false preacher O. J.
Holy, he is not pleased. It is not only that a convert might be
an indication that Hazel has been preaching the truth, O.J.'s
dishonesty is also problematical. Haze wants the truth. He wants
no phonies. "I preach there are all kinds of truth, your truth and
somebody else's but behind all of them, there's only one truth
and that is that there's no truth," he called. "No truth behind
all truths is what I and this church preach!"[45] "The truth is that

there is no truth" is a linguistic Mobius strip. This type of contradiction—self-contradiction, Christian Metz calls it—often has
an amusing effect.

> If certain contradictions are amusing, it is because they come
> very close to being reasonable statements, because they come
> within a hair's breadth of non-contradiction: for a fraction of
> a second the listener is taken in, and it is at this logical surprise
> that he will then laugh, at the contrast between the contradic-
> tory phrase and the semantically normal phrase that he had
> glimpsed or hallucinated an instant before. . . .[46]

Here is O'Connor's serious comedy at work. She parodies, she
drops one-liners, she has her characters reveal themselves inadvertently in the midst of contradiction which creates humor, but
which is also deadly serious. In fact, both the humor and the
pathos of this novel lie almost entirely in the contradictions.

Hazel is not the only self-contradictory character. Early in the
novel the reader sees Enoch, like Hazel, "looking both ways at
once."[47] After he realizes that he is going to steal the new jesus,
he backs away from Hazel and is almost hit by a taxi. The driver
asks him "how he got around so well when God had made him
by putting two backs together instead of a back and a front."[48]
The reader also learns that "Enoch's brain was divided into two
parts. The part in communication with his blood did the figuring
but it never said anything in words. The other part was stocked
up with all kinds of words and phrases."[49] Hazel's bi-directional
tendencies are echoed in these images of Enoch's double-headed-
ness. A Janus figure, Enoch looks both ways at once—toward
heaven and toward hell. (Janus, like Enoch, was a gatekeeper.)
He will make his final choice when he disappears forever into
the gorilla suit.

In the uncertain light, one of his lean white legs could be seen to disappear and then the other, one arm and then the other: a black heavier shaggier figure replaced his. For an instant, it had two heads, one light and one dark, but after a second, it pulled the dark back head over the other and corrected this.[50]

Frederick Asals points out that "Enoch's 'divided brain' is the comic counterpart of the rending split within Haze, but whereas Haze's fierce Protestant energy shapes his experience into the traditional form of the questing journey, Enoch is a kind of ur-Catholic, driven by his 'blood,' into obscure rituals which, on closer look, turn out to be parodies of biblical or Christian ceremonies."[51] These rituals are also emblematic in nature. Enoch finds the new jesus in the museum which is in the center of the park in the heart of the city—at the core, that is, of urban culture. It is dried out, impotent, and dead.

Before Enoch allows himself to approach the mummy, he goes through an elaborate ritual: watching the swimmers at the pool, eating ice cream in the stand, visiting the zoo, speaking obscenities to the animals, then proceeding on foot to the museum. This compulsive-obsessive behavior lends some sense of order to his encounter with the icon, although he does not know exactly why he finds the rituals necessary. He is preparing to face a mystery, he feels, and ordinary, casual behavior would just not be appropriate.

Enoch soon finds himself ritualistically cleaning his room, washing his furniture, buying drapes and gilt, painting the inside of the washstand, which was meant to hold a slop jar, but which would soon be the abode of the new jesus. Asals calls this washstand "Enoch's Holy of Holies, O'Connor's parody of the Ark of the Covenant."[52] At any rate, it is all emblematically appropriate. The false jesus will be set up as a slop jar in a washstand which is in the *center* of the room, the focus of Enoch's existence. "More than once after a big supper, he had dreamed of unlocking the cabinet and getting in it and then proceeding to certain rites and mysteries that he had a very vague idea about in the morning."[53]

The pictures on the wall in Enoch's room—and his later viewing of three movies—seem to be intentional echoes of an incident in *The Pilgrim's Progress* in which Christian, visiting the house of the Interpreter, is shown various emblematic tableaux and taught to interpret them. O'Connor does not parody these scenes, but as she often did with scriptural reference, she weaves similar images, situations, and meanings into her novel. The first picture the Interpreter shows Christian in *The Pilgrim's Progress* is of "a very grave person . . . with eyes lifted up to heaven, the best of books in his hand, the law of truth . . . written upon his lips, and a crown of gold . . . over his head."[54] The first picture in Enoch's room is of a moose in a lake with an irritating superior stare. The moose's eyes follow him everywhere. "He couldn't do anything in his room but what the smug face was watching." Furthermore, "he didn't know what was going to happen in his room, but when it happened, he didn't want to have the feeling that the moose was running it."[55] This moose (whose physical characteristics echo the "crowned, horned headpiece"[56] framing the mirror) broods over Enoch's room as intensely as does Bunyan's grave man, Jesus Christ, "the only man whom the Lord of the place whither thou art going hath authorized to be thy guide in all difficult places. . . ."[57] If Enoch is to become the new jesus in a gorilla suit, how appropriate that another member of the animal kingdom becomes a spiritual presence in his everyday life. Unlike Christian, however, Enoch does not find this comforting. It unsettles him most dramatically.

Bunyan's Interpreter also shows Christian a fire burning even though it is being doused with water. The Interpreter explains that the fire represents grace and it is the devil who is constantly attempting to put it out. Behind the wall, he points out, is Christ pouring oil on the fire to keep it burning. When Enoch finds himself at the movie theater, he is enticed inside by the poster of a "monster stuffing a young woman into an incinerator."[58] One of the three movies he watches is about a baboon who saves young children from burning in an orphanage. In this context, in Enoch's mind the baboon becomes linked with salvation, and in a peculiar way becomes a foreshadowing of Enoch's later disappearance into the gorilla suit and simultaneous acceptance of a self-appointed role as the new jesus. Fire becomes in *Wise Blood* the means by which the baboon saves others and in *The Pilgrim's Progress* the sign of saving grace in Jesus Christ.

Bunyan also has the Interpreter present the emblem of a man locked into a cage of despair, his heart hardened so that God's grace cannot reach it. This man in an iron cage is echoed in another movie Enoch views—a movie about life in a penitentiary, which is particularly disorienting to him. The theme of confinement and jail is also picked up in a further emblem the Interpreter shows to Christian: a man attempting to enter a castle, but having to fight his way past armed guards.

After running out of the movie theatre, Enoch runs into Hazel preaching his Church Without Christ. " 'Look at me!' Hazel Motes crie[s] with a *tare* in his throat" (italics mine).[59] The final emblem the Interpreter shows Christian in Bunyan's work is the last judgment. Hazel's tone has acquired a similar urgency, and the use of *tare* provides a final link.

> . . . then I saw the Man that sat upon the cloud open the book and bid the world draw near. Yet there was by reason of a fierce flame that issued out and came before Him, a convenient distance betwixt Him and them, as betwixt the judge and prisoners at the bar. . . . I heard it also proclaimed to them that attended on the Man that sat on the cloud, "Gather together the *tares*, the chaff and stubble, and cast them into the burning lake" (italics mine).[60]

Hazel, Enoch, the Interpreter, and Christian share a common

attraction to emblem and to the vocabulary of the Scriptures. Enoch's emblems, however, lead him not to the Celestial City, but to the ape suit. He makes a choice, buries his clothes, and adopts the physical nature of a gorilla. Many critics have viewed this as an unsatisfactory conclusion to Enoch's story—as an indicator that O'Connor has left his dilemma unresolved. I do not agree and find Leon V. Driskell and Joan T. Brittain's interpretation of this final scene particularly helpful.[61] They contend that Enoch is himself the new jesus, that the bestial nature he assumes is the only alternative the urban culture has left him. He is, literally, Yeats's rough beast from "The Second Coming," "its hour come round at last, slouching toward Bethlehem to be born."

Enoch is able to resolve his contradictions, unlike Asa Hawks and his daughter, who never do. They preach but are not believers. Asa appears blind but can see. The exact opposite of the traditional blind seer, who has insight and extrasensory knowledge, Asa is a heretic who preaches to Haze that he can save himself.[62] "That's what I already done," Haze replies, recognizing the heresy. When Haze challenges him to save his soul, Asa slams the door in his face. Even so, Asa's daughter Sabbath insists, "Anybody that blinded himself for justification ought to be able to save you. . . ."[63]

Haze's choices are never clear-cut. They are always shot through with contradiction and ambiguity. Telling the taxi driver that he has chosen to believe in nothing instead of in sin (which will lead him circuitously to Jesus), he nonetheless asks to be left at Leora Watts' house. He has chosen evil, and as he has told himself in the past, if he can choose evil, then Jesus will have a chance with him. At one point he says, "I don't need Jesus. . . . What do I need with Jesus? I got Leora Watts,"[64] but a few pages later her smile is described "as curved and sharp as the blade of a sickle,"[65] death's emblematic instrument, reminding the reader of a truth Hazel already knows: that the wages of sin is death. Haze wants a woman "not for the sake of the pleasure in her, but to prove that he didn't believe in sin since he practiced what was called it."[66] His logic here is revelatory: if he is practicing sin, then he must believe in it.[67] His route to Jesus is most stunningly indirect.

Haze insists that "blasphemy is the way to the truth . . . and there's no other way whether you understand it or not."[68] Here he is expressing one of O'Connor's favorite contentions—that the blasphemer cannot be an atheist because an atheist has nothing to blaspheme.

Haze is also disturbed by O. J. Holy's theology because it leaves no room for mystery. Everything that cannot be explained simply isn't true, O. J. Holy says. Haze reveals himself as much more Catholic than Calvinist when he decides that such rationalistic leanings are untrue. Haze demands mystery in his religion, but he also demands absolutes. When O. J. announces that in his church anyone can interpret Scripture any way they want, Haze calls him a liar.[69]

Haze's dream reveals his true discomfort with the religion he is preaching. He dreams "he was not dead but only buried. He was not waiting on the Judgment because there was no Judgment, he was waiting on nothing."[70] In his dream various people he has run into during the day look into the coffin/car in which he is trapped. They are merely curious and make no efforts to help him. Haze realizes, if only subconsciously, that if there is truly nothing rather than the Judgment, then the mundane, the everyday, superficial connections with people are all that is left. There is no such concept as the interconnectedness of humankind because the void simply swallows it up. All people do is look on suffering and need. They do not respond to it except as a curiosity. In fact, that is exactly what Haze is to the citizens of Taulkinham.

In most of O'Connor's fiction death is a major agent of revelation. This novel is no exception. From the beginning we see that

Flannery O'Connor at her autograph party for *Wise Blood* in *May, 1952.*

O'Connor Collection, Ina Dillard Russell Library, Georgia College, Milledgeville, Georgia

Hazel is closer to death than he realizes. His appearance is skull-like: "[His eyes] were the color of pecan shells and set in deep sockets. The outline of a skull under his skin was plain and insistent."[71] When he climbs into his berth on the train, he begins to remember his grandfather's coffin, and then his brother's and father's death. The berth is itself much like a coffin with one major difference: he can move. His grandfather, who had moved so rapidly over three counties, was stopped completely by death. Haze seems to fear the inability to move almost more than any-thing else, probably because when he stops moving, Jesus will be able to catch him.

As a child Haze had sneaked into a carnival side-show in which a nude woman squirmed inside a coffin, a macabre mixed image of sex and death.[72] When he returned home, he hid from his mother behind a tree, significant because Jesus was constantly moving from tree to tree in the back of his mind. How fitting then that Leora Watts, for Hazel the embodiment of illicit sex, should also be described with the metaphor of death.

Death becomes an unavoidable fact for Hazel when he murders his double. He kills him, running over him with the car, because he preaches what he doesn't believe in. " 'You ain't true,' Haze said. 'What do you get up on top of a car and say you don't believe in what you do believe in for? . . . You ain't true . . . . You believe in Jesus."[73] Of course, in this respect Hazel's words are self-convicting because he is the mirror image, the exact reversal of his double: Haze says he does believe what he doesn't really believe in. At any rate, Haze kills the man, but before he dies the two become linked forever in the sacrament of confession. The man begins to murmur:

The man was trying to say something but he was only wheez-ing. Haze squatted down by his face to listen. "Give my mother a lot of trouble," he said through a kind of bubbling in his throat. "Never giver no rest. Stole theter car. Never told the truth to my daddy or give Henry what, never give him . . ."

"You shut up," Haze said, leaning his head closer to hear the confession.

"Told where his still was and got five dollars for it," the man gasped.

"You shut up now," Haze said.

"Jesus . . ." the man said.

"Shut up like I told you to now," Haze said.

"Jesus hep me," the man wheezed.

Haze gave him a hard slap on the back and he was quiet. He leaned down to hear if he was going to say anything else but he wasn't breathing any more.[74]

Haze is father confessor—a priest hearing the final confession of a dying man. In a real sense, this man—his double—is himself, and he is witnessing his own death, as well as his own acknowledgment of sin, belief, and faith. As Kathleen Feeley puts it, "Haze knows that he has heard only one end of a dialogue and that Layfield's Redeemer truly lives."[75] This is the point at which Hazel's conversion becomes inevitable. M. Bruce Gentry has observed that "Hazel wants to learn to die, and to die more willingly than his family did."[76] This death of his double, and his recognition of his responsibility for that death, is the first climactic step in that direction.

With the loss of his car, which has enabled him to move quickly (although he never really goes anywhere), comes revelation. He rejects help and walks back to town (after the policeman has pushed the car over the edge of the cliff), buys a bucket of lime, returns to his boarding house, and blinds himself. His landlady becomes intrigued with this peculiar figure, a blind man with "the look of seeing something,"[77] a true blind seer. She knows he is totally blind because she saw him "as soon as he took off the rag he used for a while as a bandage."[78] He has become the ragged figure which he has been trying to avoid all of his life.

Just as Enoch Emery has put on the clothes of the beast, so Hazel puts on the ragged clothes of Jesus. He moves constantly, walking in his room and outside, walking with stones in his shoes, participating in the sacrament of penance.

> "Mr. Motes," the landlady said that day, when he was in her kitchen eating his dinner, "what do you walk on rocks for?"
> "To pay," he said in a harsh voice.
> "Pay for what?"
> "It don't make any difference for what," he said. "I'm paying."
> "But what have you got to show that you're paying for?" she persisted.
> "Mind your business," he said rudely. "You can't see."[79]

Though he is intentionally slower now with no car and with stones in his shoes, he is still walking, and probably to the reader it is not completely clear if he is walking toward Jesus or still attempting to escape Him.

In a letter to Louise Abbot, O'Connor explained the sacrament of penance as "not acts performed in order to attract God's attention or get credit for oneself. It is something natural that follows sorrow."[80] That is the most satisfactory way of explaining Hazel's self-mutilation. He has, for the first time in his life, felt true sorrow, and it is natural for him to handle that sorrow by attempting to reject the parts of his body that have offended him. His eye has offended him, and so he plucks it out. He blinds himself not only because he is completing an act which the false preacher Asa Hawks never finished, but also because he realizes that his vision has led him astray. If he is blind, he will no longer be able to drive. If he is blind, he will be forced to confront that image which has burned in the back of his mind all of his life. The landlady asks herself: "Why had he destroyed his eyes and saved himself unless he had some plan, unless he saw something that he couldn't get without being blind to everything else?"[81]

Richard Giannone has pointed out that in Hebrew Hazel means "He who sees God," and that Taulkinham in Greek means "the home of the small cross."[82] Hazel is finally able to see God by following the way of the cross, by confronting its scandal, and participating in the kingdom of God it ushers in. With loss, suffering, and death comes revelation. With the sacraments of confession and penance come release and redemption. In a letter to Ben Griffith, O'Connor wrote:

> Let me assure you that no one but a Catholic could have written *Wise Blood* even though it is a book about a kind of Protestant saint. It reduces Protestantism to the twin ultimate absurdities of The Church Without Christ or The Holy Church of Christ Without Christ, which no pious Protestant would do. And of course no unbeliever or agnostic could have written it because it is entirely Redemption-centered in thought. Not too many people are willing to see this, and perhaps it is hard to see because H. Motes is such an admirable nihilist. His nihilism leads him back to the fact of his Redemption, however, which is what he would have liked so much to get away from.[83]

Hazel finally gains a true convert in the landlady who "watches over" his corpse (this is *her* confrontation with death) with her eyes shut. "She sat staring with her eyes shut, into his eyes, and felt as if she had finally got to the beginning of something she couldn't begin, and she saw him moving farther and farther away, farther and farther into the darkness until he was the pin point of light."[84] Hazel is finally moving in the right direction. His death has moved him to redemption.

— 7 —

"I Don't Talk No Words":
The Violent Bear It Away

Many critics have heard an allegoric and emblematic resonance in *The Violent Bear It Away*. Martha Stephens stops short of calling the novel an allegory, but she does observe that it contains an "extensively developed allegorized conflict which . . . forms a link . . . [with] the religious literature of the distant past."[1] In his provocative study, *Flannery O'Connor's South*, Robert Coles calls Tarwater and Rayber "emblematic figures."[2] M. Bruce Gentry goes further to point out that "the allegorizing of events and characters by O'Connor's protagonists is not a device limited to a few passages; it is an essential feature of the way O'Connor's characters view the world."[3] O'Connor herself answered criticism about the novel's allegorical overtones:

> Message . . . is a bad word. It took me seven years to write *The Violent Bear It Away* and I hope there's more to it than a short story. As for its being too allegorical and all the rest, I can't agree. I wanted to get across the fact that the great Uncle (Old Tarwater) is the Christian—a sort of crypto-Catholic— and that the school teacher (Rayber) is the typical modern

man. The boy (young Tarwater) has to choose which one, which way, he wants to follow. It's a matter of vocation.[4]

The Christian, the Modern Man, the Boy—these could be characters from a morality play, or archetypes from mythology. In fact, the struggle for control and power within and among this trinity of characters pushes the novel into the realm of Christian myth. John R. May has observed that "from a hermeneutic perspective, *The Violent Bear It Away* is perhaps O'Connor's most 'complete' work—the one in which [word] fully illuminates the meaning."[5] The Word of God, spoken and silent, expressed in written Scripture and in the presence of the Logos, Jesus Christ, finds its most profound New Testament reference in the first chapter of the gospel of John: "In the beginning was the Word, and the Word was with God, and the Word was God . . . And the Word was made flesh, and dwelt among us." What follows in this first chapter of John is a description of the baptism of Jesus. John figures prominently in *The Violent Bear It Away*, as do the sacrament of baptism and the Word made flesh. In fact, what it means for words to be Worded becomes an important issue in the development of the protagonist, Francis Marion Tarwater.

The emblem which overshadows all others in *The Violent Bear It Away* is a drowning-baptism, an idea which O'Connor develops in a different way in "The River," in which a river baptism opens the kingdom of God to a child who later returns to drown in the same waters that had given him eternal life. In *The Violent Bear It Away* the child is drowned and baptized at the same instant. Unlike Harry-Bevel's baptism in "The River," Bishop's consent to or understanding of the sacrament is not an issue in the novel, especially since he is mentally retarded and incapable of understanding the ritual. For all practical purposes then, Bishop experiences something more similar to infant baptism even though he is about the same age as Harry-Bevel.

The Roman Ritual states that "if the child is in danger of death, it is to be baptized without delay."[6] In *The Violent Bear It Away* O'Connor plays with a strange reversal of this statement: the child is in danger of being baptized, so he is drowned after some delay. But Tarwater finally cannot help himself, and he pronounces the words of baptism as the child goes under the water.

This theme of baptism informs the entire book and is developed in the image patterns of water and fish, and the motif of thirst, which becomes particularly urgent in the last part of the novel. Even the landscape is strangely liquid. The old man remembers his nephew Rayber's "face . . . bobbing up and down through the corn" as he approached the cabin in an attempt to reclaim his own nephew, the baby Tarwater, whom old Tarwater had kidnapped.[7] When he was a child, Rayber had also been kidnapped and baptized by the old man, but Rayber's father had, after a few days, successfully reclaimed him. Rayber had watched his father cross the field and "he had let himself imagine that the field had an undertow that would drag his father backwards and suck him under, but he came on inexorably, only stopping every now and then to put a finger in his shoe and push out a clod of dirt."[8] Near the city, Tarwater observes a junk yard where the car bodies "seemed to be drowning into the ground, to be about half-submerged already."[9]

Bishop's eyes are described as "two pools of light,"[10] and later they are "drowned in silence."[11] On the other hand, Tarwater remembers Rayber's eyes where "knowledge moved like tree reflections in a pond where far below the surface shadows a snake may glide and disappear."[12] Water can reflect light, it can purify and refresh, but it can also conceal sin and suffocate. It is one of those images which, like the figure of Janus, looks in two directions at once, and that quality makes it particularly appropriate for this novel. Water can both baptize and it can drown.

Tarwater's problem is that he wants to be "called" as Moses, Joshua or Daniel were called—with many signs and miracles.

He does not want his first mission, much less his life purpose, to be "to baptize a dim-witted child."[13] He resists his great uncle's image of heaven as a place to receive the Bread of Life, Jesus Christ. "The boy would have a hideous vision of himself sitting forever with his great-uncle on a green bank, full and sick, staring at a broken fish and a multiplied loaf."[14] Ironically, Tarwater consents to accompany Rayber and Bishop on a fishing trip, and that is, of course, when he does his fishing for Bishop's soul—in the waters of the lake in which he both drowns and baptizes the child. It is no coincidence that the eyes of his mentor—his great-uncle—had "looked like two fish straining to get out of a net of red threads."[15] The fish Tarwater associates with life after death are caught in the waters of baptism. These waters also have the ability to quench Tarwater's profound thirst, but he decides not to drink from them.

After the drowning Tarwater's thirst becomes unassuageable. He drinks at a well, but because he is not drinking *living* water his thirst returns almost immediately. At this point, before he has fully confronted evil in the guise of the stranger in the car, Tarwater still insists that the drowning was intentional, and the baptism accidental—that because he did not *intend* to baptize, the words of baptism did not "count." "The words just come out of themselves," he says, "but it don't mean nothing."[16]

In denying the effect of the *words* of the sacrament, Tarwater is attempting to negate the efficacy of the baptism, but in so doing he unintentionally reveals his sacramentalist inclinations. Water is, of course, only half of the sacrament. Without the words, "I baptize you in the name of the Father, and of the Son, and of the Holy Spirit," there would be no baptism.[17] Tarwater attempts unsuccessfully to align himself with Rayber, for whom words are rational necessities only and contain no mystery. The old man had feared Rayber's tendency to translate all experience into "dead words,"[18] which is dramatically different from the living word, the Word of God which the child evangelist preaches.

"My Word is coming," she cries, "from the house of David, the king."[19] This Word is not only the spoken word; it is Christ Himself. Speaking of the Nativity, she asks, "Is this the Word of God, this blue-cold child?"[20]

This Word of God is sometimes even silent. Hardon notes that "not only what [Christ] said, but what he did not say, his silence, is revealing."[21] The stranger's voice which tempts Tarwater insists contrarily that God's silence is proof of God's distance and non-involvement in human affairs. "The Lord is not studying about you," the voice says to Tarwater, "don't know you exist, and wouldn't do a thing about it if He did. You're alone in the world, with only yourself to ask or thank or judge."[22] Rayber echoes these words when he attempts to teach Tarwater independence from God and intellectual self-sufficiency. "I'm the one who can save you," Rayber says.[23] In listening to Rayber, in modeling himself on the self-made man, Tarwater ostensibly abandons his calling to be a prophet of God, but his actions belie his stated inclinations. As he says, "I know what I think when I do it and when I get ready to do it, I don't talk no words. I do it."[24] Tarwater will be forced to recognize his role as a prophet after he has admitted to himself that he baptized Bishop. His involuntary action will precede his conceptualization of that act—the exact opposite of Rayber, who is most comfortable when his actions follow and support his statements of belief. Ironically, in his unintentional act of baptism, Tarwater does indeed use the words he scorns. For him word and act are ultimately unified and simultaneous.

Biblically, Tarwater's position possesses anachronistic qualities. The informing passage about New Testament prophecy is Hebrews 1:1-2. "God, who at sundry times and in divers manners spake in time past unto the fathers by the prophets, hath in these last days spoken unto us by his Son, whom he hath appointed heir of all things, by whom also he made the worlds . . . ." Significantly, when Tarwater does consider the possibility that he might actually be a prophet, he thinks in Old Testament terms and considers Old Testament models such as Elijah, Elisha, Abel, Enoch, Noah, Job, Jonah, Abraham, Moses, David, Solomon, and Habakkuk. He does not, however, omit John from his list—important because he is the one New Testament prophet who was called to prophesy the coming of the Messiah, and to baptize him.[25] The epigraph to the novel makes this connection overt: "From the days of John the Baptist until now, the kingdom of heaven suffereth violence, and the violent bear it away" (Matthew 11:12). At any rate, according to Tarwater's and his great-uncle's understanding, the proper activity for a latter-day prophet is baptism.

Of the Old Testament prophets Tarwater considers, Jonah seems to have the most influence, although the boy is also attracted to the strongly heroic figure of Elijah. Unlike Elijah, however, and much more like Jonah, Tarwater runs from his calling, fleeing God and any responsibilities he might have to assume on His behalf. At one point Tarwater hears the stranger's voice saying to him, "What you want is a sign, a real sign, suitable to a prophet. If you are a prophet, it's only right you should be treated like one. When Jonah dallied, he was cast three days in a belly of darkness and vomited up in the place of his mission."[26] This "sign" that Jonah suffered was a result of his narrowmindedness and disobedience. Tarwater's "sign"—that which will set him in the right direction (significantly, like Jonah back to dry land, or in Tarwater's case, Powderhead)—will be a homosexual rape. In this light the stranger's words are ironic and particularly sinister.

In the presence of another stranger, the truck driver, Tarwater relives the drowning of Bishop. "Sitting upright and rigid in the cab of the truck, his muscles began to jerk, his arms flailed, his mouth opened to make ways for cries that would not come. His pale face twitched and grimaced. He might have been Jonah clinging wildly to the whale's tongue."[27] Tarwater is suffocating, sinking. In reliving the drowning he himself is drowning—and in a peculiar sense, he is reliving his own baptism. Jonah's three-day immersion in water is not only a type of baptism, it is also a prefiguration of Christ's descent to the dead before his resurrection, a dying into life. Tarwater will have to confront sin in a personal way—and also see the symbol of death and resurrection on his great-uncle's grave before he will be able to find his true direction and assume his prophetic role.

Tarwater encounters many false prophets along the way, beginning with the stranger in his various guises—at first a voice in his own mind, telling him, "It ain't Jesus or the devil. It's Jesus or *you*"[28] and later manifested as the salesman Meeks who says, "Nobody owes nobody nothing."[29] The old man in the park where Tarwater almost succeeds in baptizing Bishop preaches a similar message: "Be like me, young fellow . . . don't let no jackasses tell you what to do. . . ."[30] Then there is the evil man who represents the anti-sacramental, in which the outward and visible signs of whiskey and cigarettes represent his inner corruption. After Tarwater, desperately thirsty, has drunk enough whiskey to put himself into a coma, the stranger rapes him. Tarwater's great-uncle had correctly prophesied: "You are the kind of boy . . . that the devil is always going to be offering to assist, to give you a smoke or a drink or a ride, and to ask you your bidnis. You had better mind how you take up with strangers."[31] He couldn't have come closer to the truth.[32]

The most complex false prophet, however, is Rayber, who preaches the gospel of freedom to be one's own savior. The biblical warning against false prophets is found in Matthew 7:15-20:

> Beware of false prophets, which come to you in sheep's clothing, but inwardly they are ravening wolves. Ye shall know them by their fruits. Do men gather grapes of thorns, or figs of thistles? Even so every good tree bringeth forth good fruit; but a corrupt tree bringeth forth evil fruit. A good tree cannot bring forth evil fruit, neither can a corrupt tree bring forth

good fruit. Every tree that bringeth not forth good fruit is hewn down, and cast into the fire. Wherefore by their fruits ye shall know them.

According to the old man, the fruit that Rayber brings forth is dry and seedless. After living with him for awhile, the old man concludes that Rayber's interest in his family history is not a good sign. "The old man had thought this interest in his forebears would bear fruit, but what it bore, what it bore, stench and shame, were dead words. What it bore was a dry and seedless fruit, incapable even of rotting, dead from the beginning."[33] An outward manifestation of this metaphor is Bishop, whose mental development is arrested, who cannot speak, and who ends up at the bottom of the lake.

Although Tarwater never completes the burial of his great-uncle, he chooses a spot under a fig tree for the burial site, thus providing the emblem for the biblical passage about the difference between the true and the false prophets. The old man has certainly brought forth good fruit, figs from figs, not thistles from figs. He has understood freedom in a way Rayber never has—and a way Tarwater must learn through painful means.[34] But Tarwater finally reveals himself as the good fruit that his great-uncle has brought forth.

Frederick Asals has observed that Rayber, in committing himself to rationalism, embraces a "travesty of Christianity," one in which the importance of the law is paramount. Rayber's school-teacherly role, Asals contends, echoes Galatians 3:24-25: "Wherefore the law was our schoolmaster to bring us unto Christ, that we might be justified by faith. But after faith is come, we are no longer under a schoolmaster."[35]

In a letter in which she discusses the title of the novel, O'Connor speaks of "the violence of love, of giving more than the law demands."[36] The stranger's voice, in whatever guise it appears, is completely self-centered. It gives of itself to no one. During the rare times it urges moral choices upon Tarwater, it goes not one iota beyond the minimum requirements of the law.[37]

> And as for Judgment Day, the stranger said, every day is Judgment Day . . . . Ain't you old enough to have learnt that yet for yourself? Don't everything you do, everything you have ever done, work itself out right or wrong before your eye and usually before the sun has set?[38]

Tarwater has discovered already that civil law is insurmountable. On a trip to the city with his great-uncle, he visits lawyer after lawyer, his great-uncle arguing with each one of them about the entailment of his property. "My Lord!" Tarwater cries, ". . . Ain't you got any sense? They all tell you the same thing. It's only one law and it's nothing you can do about it. I got sense enough to get that; why ain't you?"[39] Civil law, like God's law, cannot be changed. It is rigid and immutable. Tarwater asks his great-uncle why, after he was kidnapped, Rayber had not repeatedly tried to reclaim him. "'Why didn't he bring the law out here and get me back?' he had asked. 'You want to know why?' his uncle said. 'Well I'll tell you why. I'll tell you exactly why. It was because he found you a heap of trouble. He wanted it all in his head. You can't change a child's pants in your head.' "[40] Rayber will neither go beyond the requirements of the law to reclaim the child, nor will he use the civil law to get him back. Only love could motivate him so to act. That the gospel of love in Jesus Christ is the fulfillment of the law is a Christian commonplace—but it is one to which Rayber has not yet committed himself.

The world of grace in *The Violent Bear It Away* is a world charged with the grandeur of God.[41] It is a world in which the four elements of the ancient world—earth, fire, water, and air—are inextricably entwined. All metaphoric, allegoric, and emblematic meanings which are derived from any one of these elements impinge on all of the other elements. We have already seen how in this novel O'Connor describes the landscape, the earth, as if it were liquid. In O'Connor's stories the red Georgia clay is frequently associated with the earthly kingdom and the stuff of life. The source is, of course, Genesis, in which God creates Adam from the dust of the earth. The novel begins with a reference to earth.

> Francis Marion Tarwater's uncle had been dead for only half a day when the boy got too drunk to finish digging his grave and a Negro named Buford Munson, who had come to get a jug filled, had to finish it and drag the body from the breakfast table where it was still sitting and bury it in a decent and Christian way, with the sign of its Savior at the head of the grave and enough dirt on top to keep the dogs from digging it up.

This association of earth and the cross is important. Tarwater must confront the fact of his own fallenness, his own propensity to sin, and his human position as a victim of sin before he can be fully redeemed, before he can smear over his forehead a handful of dirt from his uncle's grave. Albert Sonnenfeld has noted the movement from literal to symbolic action in O'Connor's stories, observing that in this instance Tarwater is wearing the Ash Wednesday mark of repentance on his forehead. Sonnenfeld says further that "for Flannery O'Connor, the Word always leads to the Act."[42] As Tarwater moves from a literal to a symbolic understanding of the earth, he also begins to see that he must assume his role as prophet; he must act. The earth, the red clay which anchors him to the earth in his sinfulness, also becomes the sign of redemption. The gaping, unfilled grave of the first chapter—Tarwater's unfinished act which has haunted him— was, unbeknownst to him, finished by someone else the day Tarwater began the task. Once Tarwater discovers that the corpse of his great-uncle has not been burned, that in fact it has been buried under the sign of the cross, the boy is released from his guilt. Earth, then, which receives the body, also symbolically releases it. It is appropriate that Tarwater smears this same dirt on his forehead.

Just as earth both restrains and releases, as water both baptizes and drowns, so fire in *The Violent Bear It Away* both purifies and destroys. Tarwater is as attracted to fire as he is to water, using it, in fact, in similar ways. He drowns Bishop (in water described as "white fire"[43]) as he believes he has burned the corpse of his great-uncle—out of anger and spite, and as an expression of his freedom from God. One of the protean forms of the devil-tempter-stranger is Mr. Meeks, who, appropriately, sells copper flues and considers using Tarwater in his business. Tarwater has other things on his mind, however. The memory of the fire he has set is strong as he gazes at the night sky bright with the lights of the city.

"Look," Tarwater said suddenly, sitting forward, his face close to the windshield, "we're headed in the wrong direction. We're going back where we came from. There's the fire again. There's the fire we left!"

Ahead of them in the sky there was a faint glow, steady, and not made by lightning. "That's the same fire we came from!" the boy said in a high voice.

"Boy, you must be nuts," the salesman said. "That's the city we're coming to. That's the glow from the city lights. I reckon this is your first trip anywhere."

"You're turned around," the child said; "it's the same fire."[44]

Tarwater feels he is going in the wrong direction, running from one fire straight into another one, and in a sense that is exactly what he is doing, but it is, of course, directly to his destiny as the baptizer that he is running, which is not the wrong direction at all, but the right one. This will be a difficult and painful experience for him. His eyes will appear "scorched"[45] after the rape, but he will return to Powderhead to set fire to the tree, his own "burning bush," a sign from God.

Without air, the fourth element, there can be no fire, and although it is not as pervasive an image as the elements of water, earth, and fire, it is an important theme at the end of the novel. Air is connected with breath. Early in the novel, when Rayber returns to attempt to reclaim the baby, the welfare-woman "let out her breath slowly as if she were releasing the last patience on earth."[46] Later, in the middle of his "conversation" with the stranger's voice, the sun, so often connected with Christ and redemption, is described as being "directly overhead, apparently dead still, holding its breath."[47] When Tarwater is drunk, he imagines that the sky is "lowering, coming down fast to smother him."[48] The stranger himself emits a sigh "like a gust of sand raised and dropped suddenly by the wind."[49]

Breath and wind are traditionally associated with the Holy Spirit. In these examples the breath is ineffective, even dead. The smothering sensation Tarwater feels is even a foreshadowing of the drowning he will commit. Air, then, is associated with a lack of breath, an absence of the Holy Spirit, but also with an enlivening process. After Tarwater's rape, as he approaches the old homestead, a breeze begins to stir.[50] "He felt a breeze on his neck as light as a breath and he half-turned, sensing that some one stood behind him . . . . The presence was as pervasive as an odor, a warm sweet body of air encircling him. . . ."[51] He is soon to confront the cross on his great-uncle's grave and enter the land of the living once again.

Of course, the cross contains its own double meaning.[52] An instrument of torture, it is also the sign of salvation. The old man speaks often "of the sweat and stink of the cross."[53] After his great-uncle's death, Tarwater decides not to set up a cross on his grave. "I'll be too wore out to set up any cross. I ain't bothering with trifles,"[54] he says, in intentional blasphemy. The stranger argues that the cross would rot by Judgment Day anyway. But in spite of his intentions, Tarwater has been marked by the sign of the cross forever. When his great-uncle tells him about his baptism, "the boy would move his thin shoulder blades irritably as if he were shifting the burden of Truth like a cross on his back."[55] Later when he is drunk, "his cheekbones protruded, narrow and thin like the arms of a cross."[56] When he discovers the cross which Buford Munson has set up on the grave, despite the boy's own intentions of not burying his great-uncle under the sign of the cross, he appears to stare "downward at the cross as if they followed below the surface of the earth to where its roots encircled all the dead."[57] The implication is that the love of the cross was infused in Tarwater's soul at his baptism, and there is nothing he can do to rid himself of it. Hardon explains the phenomenon of sacramental character this way:

> There is something so mysteriously transcendent about three of the sacraments that they radically and permanently change the person who receives them by an immutable participation in Christ's priesthood. He remains unalterably baptized, or confirmed, or ordained, no matter what else may happen to his holiness in the sight of God. He thus retains an enduring substratum of union with God that needs only to be activated to rise from its dormant state.[58]

Rayber continually fights this "substratum of union with God." He experiences uncontrollable rushes of love for Bishop—"horrifying love," he calls it.[59] "It was love without reason, love for something futureless, love that appeared to exist only to be itself, imperious and all demanding, the kind that would cause him to make a fool of himself in an instant. And it only began with Bishop. It began with Bishop and then like an avalanche covered everything his reason hated."[60] As a result, Rayber views himself as divided into two parts, the violent and the rational. His violent side loves; his rational side does not. In like manner he establishes a dichotomy between baptism and intelligence, thus linking baptism with violence, prefiguring Tarwater's action on Bishop. Tarwater himself had experienced two separate baptisms—one performed in love by the old man and one performed on his buttocks in parody of the rite by Rayber. Asals calls this latter "a demonic consecration which, like a promissory note, will be collected many pages later by the homosexual rapist."[61] These two baptisms represent Tarwater's eventual alternative choices. In fact, in attempting to deny the efficacy of the old man's baptism, he almost necessitates the rape, which will in its own violent way allow him to receive revelation.

Although Rayber and Tarwater may appear to be opposites, they are more alike than either one would ever admit. Rayber realizes that he cannot look Bishop in the eye without experiencing irresistible love, so he feels that likewise Tarwater needs to train himself to look Bishop in the eye in order to consciously resist baptizing him. Rayber's choice is between love and reason; Tarwater's is between baptism and drowning. Love and baptism are inextricably linked.

Like Hamlet, Tarwater cannot immediately bring himself to act. "I mean to wait and see what happens,"[62] he rationalizes at one point. " 'And suppose nothing don't happen?' Meeks asked. . . . 'Then I'll make it happen . . . . I can act.' "[63] When Tarwater finally gets his chance to act, to choose to drown the child, thereby absolutely affirming death over life, he cannot carry through. He baptizes Bishop. As Miles Orvell says, "He does NO, but he *says* YES."[64] Rayber had attempted to drown the child at one time, but he could not finally carry through, and he dragged the child out of the water to be resuscitated. Tarwater drowns the child, but chooses at the last minute to save him eternally.

It is important for Tarwater to learn that he does not have

complete control of his destiny. He can make choices, good and bad, but finally what happens to him, the way people respond to him and act upon him, the direction God leads him, are beyond his control. This is a truth the rape painfully demonstrates to him. Kathleen Feeley has said that with this event Tarwater "learns that being acted upon, as well as acting, is an intrinsic part of living. His passivity in the violent evil that is perpetrated on him renders that evil no less real, just as his willing only subconsciously the words of baptism in no way negates their reality."[65]

His hunger, like his thirst, is also uncontrollable. This is both a spiritual *and* physical phenomenon that is heavily emblematic, and finally, at the end of the novel Tarwater begins to understand it.

> The boy remained standing there, his still eyes reflecting the field the Negro had crossed. It seemed to him no longer empty but peopled with a multitude. Everywhere, he saw dim figures seated on the slope and as he gazed he saw that from a single basket the throng was being fed. His eyes searched the crowd for a long time as if he could not find the one he was looking for. Then he saw him. The old man was lowering himself to the ground. When he was down and his bulk had settled, he leaned forward, his face turned toward the basket, impatiently following its progress toward him. The boy too leaned forward, aware at last of the object of his hunger, aware that it was the same as the old man's and that nothing on earth would fill him. His hunger was so great that he could have eaten all the loaves and fishes after they were multiplied.[66]

His hunger then becomes a flood. "He felt it rising in himself through time and darkness, rising through the centuries, and he knew that it rose in a line of men whose lives were chosen to sustain it, who would wander in the world, strangers from that violent country where the silence is never broken except to shout the truth."[67] O'Connor frequently said that for the hard of hearing one must shout. Rayber, for one, had often chosen silence, switching off his hearing aid when he wanted uncomfortable truths to be excluded. In our last glimpse of him, he has just turned his hearing aid on to capture Bishop's bellowing as he is drowned. "The machine made the sounds seem to come from inside him as if something in him were tearing itself free,"[68] O'Connor writes. The truth is bellowed—shouted—to him before descending to silence.

Significantly, walking through the streets of the city with Bishop and Rayber, Tarwater had felt the silence speak to him. The silence had told him to baptize the child. At the end of the novel he heeds words "as silent as seeds opening one at a time in his blood."[69] The silence speaks, the drowning saves, the fire purifies and destroys, the cross tortures and redeems. Tarwater once again sets out toward the city, this time to shout the Word of God to those who are sleeping, to those who will probably never hear him.

— 8 —

O'Connor's Postmodern Story:
"Judgement Day"

O'Connor's editor, Robert Giroux, received "Judgement Day" in early July, 1964, a month before her death.[1] In May she had written to him that she had been working on the story intermittently for several years.[2] Essentially a revision of "The Geranium," O'Connor's first published story, "Judgement Day" may not conclude O'Connor's writing career as neatly as some critics have suggested. Perhaps, knowing she did not have long to live, she hurried her revisions, especially since she was also trying to complete *Everything That Rises Must Converge*, which was published posthumously. Writing to Catharine Carver from the hospital where her lupus was clearly out of control, O'Connor indicated on June 17th that she was not yet satisfied with the story.[3] Ten days later in a letter to Janet McKane, O'Connor wrote that she was "doing a lot of necessary rewriting on old stories and today in bed I did a day's work. This must be the result of my friends' prayers."[4] On the same day she wrote again to Catharine Carver:

> Will you look at this one ["Judgement Day"] and say if you think it fitten for the collection or if you think it can be made

so? It's a rewrite of a story that I have had around since 1946 and never been satisfied with, but I hope I have it now except for details maybe.[5]

By July 15th she was beginning her revisions based on Carver's suggestions, and she sent "Parker's Back" to her with the comment that she thought "it's much better than the last ["Judgement Day"]. . . ."[6]

It seems clear from these comments that she was still not completely satisfied with the story. Perhaps it is no coincidence, then, that this is one of the only stories in the collection that omits symbolic or literal reference to the gospel and to conversion (which she had said earlier was the only true theme of any story). Inside the apartment in the middle of a northern city, the tree line and its connections with Christ are as distant as the South itself. Most significantly, the sun is obscured—if not by buildings, then by the weather. In O'Connor's fiction if the sun is absent, the Son is also missing. The story seems peculiarly and atypically devoid of emblem. While this could explain her lingering dissatisfaction with the story, it may also suggest a new direction for O'Connor—one that she did not live to explore.[7]

That the meaning of language is often indeterminate, difficult, ambiguous, and even self-contradictory is a concept that raises issues at the heart of poststructuralist literary theory. Terry Eagleton explains this phenomenon, pointing out that language is inordinately slippery—"a much less stable affair than the classical structuralists had considered." He continues:

Instead of being a well-defined, clearly demarcated structure containing symmetrical units of signifiers and signifieds, it now begins to look much more like a sprawling limitless web where there is a constant interchange and circulation of elements, where none of the elements is absolutely definable and where everything is caught up and traced through by everything else.[8]

O'Connor seems to suggest something similar about language in this story—in the way she handles dialogue, in the way the characters interpret each other's discourse, and in Tanner's final "revelation," which is much more ambiguous than any of her other characters' similar experiences.

O'Connor begins the story with dramatic irony, a device she uses frequently in her fiction—but here it is particularly significant because of the emphasis in this story on the difficulties of interpretation.

> Tanner was conserving all his strength for the trip home. He meant to walk as far as he could get and trust to the Almighty to get him the rest of the way. That morning and the morning before, he had allowed his daughter to dress him and had conserved that much more energy.[9]

At this point in the story the reader does not know just how far the journey home will be for Tanner, but it is clear to the reader that if Tanner is so incapacitated that he must have his daughter dress him, then he will not be going very far. Tanner has not interpreted his situation this way at all. In fact, although he plans on literally "getting home" to Georgia, he will instead succeed in metaphorically "getting home."

Tanner views his daughter as the only real obstacle between himself and home. One of her characteristic activities is talking to herself. Shortly after Tanner arrived in the city from Georgia, he learned that she did not mean for him to enter into these "dialogues." "That had not been wanted," O'Connor writes. "She glowered at him as if, old fool that he was, he should still have had sense enough not to answer a woman talking to herself.

She questioned herself in one voice and answered herself in another."[10] The daughter's discourse is ostensibly self-referential, so in his first error of answering a question directed not to him, but back to the questioner herself, Tanner demonstrates his naive assumption that he can interpret the discourse of this new culture he has entered. He discovers that he is wrong. He has entered Eagleton's "sprawling limitless web."

Ready to set out on his journey home, he puts a note in his pocket with specific and detailed instructions on what to do with his body should he die on the way. If the spoken word becomes impossible, he feels that the written word will carry authority and meaning. In fact, Tanner has realized that his daughter intends to ignore his spoken wishes about being buried back home. Again, Eagleton's comments are helpful.

> If objects and events in the real world are experienced as lifeless and alienated [which they always are in O'Connor's city world], if history seems to have lost direction and lapsed into chaos, it is always possible to put all of this 'in brackets,' 'suspend the referent' and take words as your object instead.[11]

Recall the message Tanner wrote to Coleman in his only letter home: "This place is alrite if you like it. Yours truly, W. T. Tanner."[12] "This place is alrite," he begins, and he sounds positive if understated in his response. But the "if you like it" says much more. If you don't like it, then it is not all right. Does he like it or not? He is not committing himself, although the implication is that he is superior to any involvement in it. His writing, "turning in on itself," defers meaning in the deconstructionist sense.

Other contradictions and interpretive difficulties arise throughout the story. In an altercation between Tanner's daughter and her husband, the difference between their definitions of the word *nigger*—and the cultural understandings, expectations, and connotations associated with these definitions—are pronounced.

"My daddy is here to stay," his daughter said. "He ain't going to last long. He was somebody when he was somebody. He never worked for nobody in his life but himself and had people—other people—working for him."

"Yah? Niggers is what he had working for him," the son-in-law said. "That's all. I've worked a nigger or two myself."

"Those were just nawthun niggers you worked," she said, her voice suddenly going lower so that Tanner had to lean forward to catch the words. "It takes brains to work a real nigger. You got to know how to handle them."[13]

Here culture reveals itself in speech and sign. The same word—*nigger*—takes on different associations and a set of different, even contradictory social meanings. This difference, and Tanner's blindness to it, will result in a fatal act of violence.

Tanner is confident of his ability to "understand" Negroes, and in his home setting he has devised a set of ritualistic questions, phrases and actions which establish his relationship with the black race—a relationship which is threatening but clear. Tanner whittles with a knife and says, "Nigger, this knife is in my hand now but if you don't quit wasting my time and money, it'll be in your gut shortly."[14] The Negroes obey him and later they pick up his crude carvings and take them home. When Coleman arrives, Tanner has to modify the ritual; to establish his control over Coleman, he must be more creative. Crude carvings and predictable phrasing will not work because Coleman's presence requires another sign and another language. He is clearly a threat to Tanner's authority, and when on the second day of his brooding presence, the workers break for lunch a half hour early, Tanner realizes he must do something; he must somehow establish himself as sign-giver, if he is to maintain control. He walks over to Coleman, his whittling knife working as usual on a stray piece of wood, and begins without realizing it to carve a pair of glasses. When he finishes, he gives them to Coleman, calls him "Preacher," and asks him whether he sees a black man or a white man when he looks through them. When Coleman answers, "He's white," Tanner has succeeded in forcing him to define the parameters of their relationship. The differences between white and black pronounced, they now enter a stage of extended symbiosis. For thirty years they live together, Coleman "a negative image"[15] of Tanner. Tanner never articulates this, of course. In fact, his similarity to Coleman is apparent to him only in brief flashes, which he largely ignores. Tanner's ritualistic social encounter with the Negroes involves language and sign (the knife, the carvings, the glasses). In fact, that signs in themselves create a language is what Julia Kristeva has described as "a general social law . . . the symbolic dimension which is given in language . . . every social practice offer[ing] a specific expression of that law." She says further that

> what semiotics has discovered in studying "ideologies" (myths, rituals, moral codes, arts, etc.) as sign systems is that the *law* governing or, if one prefers, *the major constraint* affecting any social practice, lies in the fact that it signifies, i.e. that it is articulated *like* a language. Every social practice, as well as being the object of external (economic, political, etc.) determinations, is also determined by a set of signifying rules, by virtue of the fact that there is present an order of language. . . .[16]

When he moves to the city and encounters a Negro in the same building, it is clear that Tanner does not understand the signifying rules, which are different in the city. He speaks one language, but the Negro actor hears another. Tanner expects the actor to react as Coleman would have, and he assumes from the beginning that because he himself is from the South, and the actor is a Negro which Tanner associates with the South, he and the actor will be able to relate to one another. Desperately lonely,

Tanner makes very calculated opening moves in the Negro's direction, but the speech formula, the sign system, which worked in the South, does not work in the city. In fact, Tanner finds himself being interpreted in an unexpected way. In the South the Negroes understand the subtext of his banter, but in the North, when he says to the actor, "I thought you might know somewhere around here we could find us a pond, Preacher," the actor hears only racial insult and responds, "And I'm not no preacher! I'm not even no Christian. I don't believe that crap. There ain't no Jesus and there ain't no God."[17] Tanner replies, "And you ain't black . . . and I ain't white," and the Negro slams him against the wall. Tanner's response to blasphemy is to reassert the social rules that have sustained him and given him a sense of place and power in the past. But they are not effective in this new setting.

The social rules are different, the order of language is turned upside down, and the result for Tanner is that he suffers a stroke which paralyzes his tongue. He cannot speak, and communication with his daughter, which had been difficult before, now becomes almost impossible. Interpretation—or rather, misinterpretation—becomes a major source of conflict. Earlier in the narrative she had complained, "He wanted to come and now he's here, he don't like it," but the next paragraph makes completely clear that "he had not wanted to come."[18] Likewise, before he left the South, Tanner had been advised by the black doctor that his daughter "don't want no old daddy like you . . . . Maybe she say she do, but that ain't likely."[19] Now when Tanner dreams of going home in a coffin, he dreams not of his death, but of his resurrection into his old life. Notice that he possesses no real sense of eschatology. He uses an eschatological *language* of death, judgment, and the last things, and in fact any moral sense he has developed is a direct consequence of his fear of hell, but in his own imagining of death, he moves not forward toward the Day of Judgment, but backward toward his life in the South,

where "Judgement Day! Judgement Day!" is his excited cry of
greeting as he bursts out of the coffin to meet an astonished
Coleman. Judgment Day, in other words, contains no judgment
for him personally, although he is certain that it will have meaning for his daughter.

> "The Judgement is coming," he muttered. "The sheep'll be
> separated from the goats. Them that kept their promises from
> them that didn't. Them that did the best they could with what
> they had from them that didn't. Them that honored their
> father and their mother from them that cursed them. . . ."[20]

When he begins his journey home, shuffling slowly from chair
to wall to door, he suddenly has insight. "A sensation of terror
and defeat swept over him. He would never make it. He would
never get there dead or alive."[21] It is snowing heavily outside,
and it is clear to the reader that he will not make it, but he
perseveres anyway. Reaching the stairwell, he collapses, and in
his delirium he remembers his dream and imagines that Coleman
is bending over him, astonished at his resurrection. In reality,
the Negro actor and his wife stand watching, listening to Tanner
yell, "Judgement Day! Judgement Day! You idiots didn't know
it was Judgement Day, did you?" The actor does not take this
apparently fresh insult lightly. To make matters worse, Tanner
looks at him and says, "Coleman?" and the actor thinks he is
calling him "coal man." In this postmodern world, Tanner's intentions mean nothing. The Negro interprets the signs as he reads
them, and his interpretation of yet another insult leads to the
act of murder.

Is there a gospel in this text? Is there conversion? Tanner does
come to the realization that he should have done everything in
his power to remain in the South, that he should have forgotten
his pride and worked for the black doctor, the only way he could
have remained in his home. Tanner's daughter, we learn in the

final paragraph, eventually sends her father's body home to Georiga—but the kind of revelation that uncovers the meaning of the incarnation (as in "Parker's Back") or the significance of sacrament (as in "The River") or the surprise of grace (as in "A Good Man Is Hard to Find") is not present in this story. The conclusion is ambiguous. In "A Good Man Is Hard to Find" the grandmother's vision clears long enough for her to see the relationship between The Misfit and her son, Bailey. It is not just that The Misfit wears Bailey's shirt. The grandmother's "mistaken" identification of The Misfit as one of her own babies is actually a revelation—a sign of the interconnectedness of all of humankind. In "Judgement Day" Tanner's mistaken identification of the actor as Coleman does not lead to the same conclusion. Tanner's whole problem has been that he has assumed all along that Coleman and the Negro actor across the hall were similar, although they could not have been more different. In fact, the actor seems to have much more in common with Tanner's daughter who has also rejected God. What Tanner "sees," then, is not the truth, but an impossibility. Coleman and the actor are not linked. There are no connections between them.

The city has removed from humanity the interdependencies Tanner had experienced in the South. In fact, Tanner's daughter explicitly defines life in the city as solitary, nasty, and short.

"You keep away from them. Don't you go over there trying to get friendly with him. They ain't the same around here and I don't want any trouble with niggers, you hear me? If you have to live next to them, just you mind your business and they'll mind theirs. That's the way people were meant to get along in this world. Everybody can get along if they just mind their business. Live and let live . . . . Up here everybody minds their own business and everybody gets along."[22]

When his daughter returns to the apartment, she discovers

Tanner dead, "his head and arms thrust between the spokes of the banister; his feet dangled over the stairwell like those of a man in the stocks."[23] He has violated the social rules of the culture into which he has been transplanted, and his punishment has been not only public humiliation, Puritan style, but death. The urban moral law, based on a certain code of behavior, has condemned him because he has not understood its signifiers. Unlike the typical O'Connor character, Tanner has not gained any final insight into the meaning of the Word incarnate.

He has not been discharged from the law. He experiences no revelation because in this city world there is no gospel. Remember that at the end of *The Violent Bear It Away* Tarwater set his face "toward the dark city, where the children of God lay sleeping." In a letter to "A," O'Connor indicates that "the children of God I daresay will dispatch him pretty quick."[24] The prophet is drawn to the city, but the city has no ears to hear him.

Is Tanner a prophet? He brings with him warnings of hell and judgement, but even though Tanner's final statements about "going home" contain a biblical resonance, at no point do we see that Tanner really understands what this means. O'Connor has presented a postmodern prophet in a postChristian story in which allegory cannot function, emblem is nonexistent or ambiguous, and even eschatology becomes abstract, impersonal, and strangely irrelevant. Tanner is a strong character, and the story is compelling, but in it O'Connor seems to have shifted her vision. She sees no room for revelation in the wasteland of modern urban culture.

Flannery O'Connor is prophetically speaking a language that will make most sense to literary theorists of the 1980's, where, to repeat Eagleton's words, "everything is caught up and traced through by everything else" because there is no "well-defined, clearly demarcated structure containing symmetrical units of signifiers and signifieds." O'Connor would not have put it that way, of course. She would have been cautious—probably even impatient with current literary theory (she once said that she was "congenitally innocent of theory, but [had] certain preoccupations"[25]) but that is because any theory which lost sight of the Incarnation would be for her seriously incomplete.

"Recover your simplicity," O'Connor once wrote to a friend who had gone too far with Freudian theory. Be properly scared, she would advise us. But at the same time, she would gaze unflinchingly into the face of modern culture and write what she saw. In *Wise Blood* the new jesus found an identity in the gorilla suit—the rough beast slouching toward Bethlehem to be born. In"Judgement Day" there seems to be no operative Jesus at all. Of course, the story must be seen in the context of her entire opus—and particularly in the context of her two other final stories—"Parker's Back" and "Revelation." Viewed in this way, "Judgement Day" is no less bleak, but it does provide an alternative view, not necessarily O'Connor's final and definitive statement. That O'Connor would allow this darker vision to find expression says much about her courage. It also shows her still straddling the two kingdoms just as she was preparing to step over the brink to leave this one behind forever.

Notes

Chapter One

[1]*The Habit of Being*, ed. Sally Fitzgerald (New York: Vintage Books, 1979), p. 508. For other published letters see also *The Correspondence of Flannery O'Connor and the Brainard Cheneys*, ed. C. Ralph Stephens (Jackson: University Press of Mississippi, 1986).
[2]Ibid., p. 586.
[3]Ibid., p. 90.
[4]Ibid., p. 184.
[5]Ibid., p. 163.
[6]Ibid., p. 280.
[7]Ibid., p. 285.
[8]Ibid., p. 340.
[9]Ibid., p. 310.
[10]Ibid., p. 473.
[11]Ibid., pp. 80-81.
[12]Ibid., p. 259.
[13]Ibid., p. 27.
[14]Ibid., p. 417.
[15]Ibid., p. 248.
[16]Ibid., p. 219.
[17]Ibid., p. 188.
[18]Ibid., p. 239.
[19]Ibid., p. 295.
[20]Ibid., p. 300.
[21]Ibid., p. 242.
[22]Ibid., p. 458.
[23]In one of the books in her personal library (Jacques Maritain, *Art and Scho-*

lasticism: With Other Essays), O'Connor underlined the following passage: "Do not make the absurd attempt to sever in yourself the artist and the Christian. They are one, if you really *are* a Christian, and if your art is not isolated from your soul by some aesthetic system. But apply only the artist in you to the work in hand; precisely because they are one, the work will be as wholly of the one as of the other" [Arthur Kinney, *Flannery O'Connor's Library: Resources of Being* (Athens: University of Georgia Press, 1985), p. 94].

[24]*The Habit of Being*, p. 304.

[25]Ibid., p. 338.

[26]Ibid., p. 160.

[27]Ibid., p. 100.

[28]Ibid., pp. 346-47.

[29]Ibid., p. 347.

[30]Ibid., p. 479.

[31]Ibid., p. 354.

[32]Ibid., p. 476.

[33]Ibid., p. 307.

[34]Ibid.

[35]Ibid., p. 430.

[36]Ibid., p. 452.

[37]Ibid., p. 229.

[38]Ibid.

[39]Ibid., p. 227.

[40]Ibid., p. 302.

[41]Ibid., p. 407.

[42]Ibid., p. 354.

[43]Ibid., p. 436.

[44]Ibid., p. 437.

[45]Ibid., p. 582.

[46]Ibid., p. 411.

[47]Ibid., p. 159.

[48]Ibid., p. 416.

[49]Ibid., p. 343.

[50]Ibid., p. 596.

Chapter Two

[1]Review of Paul Horgan, *Humble Powers: Three Novelettes* in *The Presence of Grace and Other Book Reviews*, compiled by Leo J. Zuber, ed. Carter W. Martin (Athens: University of Georgia Press, 1983), p. 19.

[2]Josephine Hendin, *The World of Flannery O'Connor* (Bloomington: Indiana University Press, 1970), p. 28. Hendin takes the phrase "comic literalization" from F.W. Dupee.

[3]Peter M. Daly, *Literature in the Light of the Emblem* (Toronto: University of Toronto Press, 1979), p. 168. Daly is quoting David J. Alpaugh, "Emblem and Interpretation in *The Pilgrim's Progress*," *English Literary History*, 33 (1966), p. 300. In O'Connor's personal library is Mario Praz's *The Flaming Heart: Essays on Crashaw, Machiavelli, and Other Studies in the Relations Between Italian and*

English Literature from Chaucer to T.S. Eliot (New York: Doubleday, 1958). Praz describes the seventeenth-century world view in terms which O'Connor must have found appealing. "All the phenomena of the surrounding world, all the categories of learning, supplied them with suggestions for this mental idiosyncrasy of theirs: they discovered mysterious witticisms in the aspects of the earth and the sky, heroical devices and symbols in all the creatures; animals and plants possessed a witty language for them; and full of wit was the language of god; for since man fashions God in his own image, and a cannibal imagines God as a man-eater, so a seventeenth-century man had an idea of God as a witty speaker, who, talking in riddles to Men and angels, clothed his most exalted concepts with various heroical Devices, and pictorial Symbols" (p. 206. Quote taken from E. Tesauro, *Il Cannocchiale Aristotelico*, Venice, 1655, p. 61.).

[4]*Literature in the Light of the Emblem*, p. 61.

[5]*English Emblem Books* (London: Chatto and Windus, 1948; reprinted. New York: Octagon Books, 1966), p. 4.

[6]William James, *The Varieties of Religious Experience: A Study in Human Nature* (New York: Crowell-Collier, 1961), p. 56.

[7]David Eggenschwiler, *The Christian Humanism of Flannery O'Connor* (Detroit: Wayne State University Press, 1972), p. 13. See also John Hawkes, "Flannery O'Connor's Devil," *Critical Essays on Flannery O'Connor*, ed. Melvin J. Friedman and Beverly Lyon Clark (Boston: G.K. Hall, 1985), pp. 92-100, reprinted from *Sewanee Review*, 70 (1962), pp. 395-407.

[8]See "On Her Own Work," *Mystery and Manners*, ed. Sally and Robert Fitzgerald (New York: Farrar, Straus & Giroux, 1969), p. 111. In O'Connor's library one finds Barry Ulanov's *Sources and Resources: The Literary Tradition of Christian Humanism* (Westminster, MD: Newman Press, 1960). Ulanov's description of modern allegory is pertinent here: "The first level, the literal, of modern allegory will be quite different, must be, from the letter of medieval and Renaissance writing. But the second and third and fourth planes—those that go to make up the spirit of any allegorical communication—should obviously be the same for Christian writers and readers in this not-so-clearly Christian era as it was in that time so unmistakably concerned to emulate the ministry and passion and death and resurrection of Christ, and to understand those who loved Him and those who did not, and to make sense of those who followed after Him and those who did not" (pp. 8-9).

[9]*Ibid.*, pp. 75-76.

[10]*The Sewanee Review*, 63 (Spring 1955), p. 204.

[11]Maureen Quilligan, *The Language of Allegory: Defining the Genre* (Ithaca, NY: Cornell University Press, 1979), p. 223.

[12]Thomas Linehan, "Anagogical Realism in Flannery O'Connor," *Renascence* 37 (Winter 1985), 94.

[13]"The Geranium," *The Complete Stories of Flannery O'Connor* (New York: Farrar, Straus & Giroux, 1971), p. 6.

[14]Ibid., p. 3.

[15]Ibid., p. 6.

[16]Ibid., p. 14.

[17]"The Barber," *The Complete Stories of Flannery O'Connor,* p. 21.

[18]"The Crop," *The Complete Stories of Flannery O'Connor,* p. 33.

[19]Ibid., p. 34.

[20]"Writing Short Stories," *Mystery and Manners,* pp. 87-88.

[21]Frederick Asals has noted the influence of Faulkner in her other early stories. See his *Flannery O'Connor: The Imagination of Extremity* (Athens: University of Georgia Press, 1982), pp. 10, 16.

[22]"The Turkey," *The Complete Stories of Flannery O'Connor,* p. 45.

[23]Ibid., p. 46.

[24]Ibid.

[25]Ibid., p. 47.

[26]Ibid.

[27]Ibid., p. 49.

[28]Ibid., p. 51.

[29]Ibid., p. 53.

[30]"Good Country People," *The Complete Stories of Flannery O'Connor,* p. 271.

[31]Ibid., p. 274.

[32]Ibid., p. 273.

[33]Ibid., p. 279.

[34]Ibid., p. 273.

[35]Ibid., p. 276.

[36]Ibid., p. 288.

[37]Ibid., p. 285.

[38]Ibid., p. 287.

[39]Ibid., p. 289.

[40]Ibid., p. 287.

[41]Ibid., p. 290.

[42]Ibid., p. 291.

[43]"The Life You Save May Be Your Own," *The Complete Stories of Flannery O'Connor,* p. 147.

[44]Ibid., p. 148.

[45]George Ferguson, *Signs and Symbols in Christian Art* (New York: Oxford University Press, 1954), p. 45. See also Stuart L. Burns, "'Torn by the Lord's Eye': Flannery O'Connor's Use of Sun Imagery," *Twentieth Century Literature,* 13 (1967).

[46]"The Life You Save May Be Your Own," *The Complete Stories of Flannery O'Connor,* p. 146.

[47]Ibid., p. 145.

[48]Ibid., p. 153.

[49]Ibid., p. 155.

[50]Ibid., p. 156.

[51]Ibid., p. 149.

[52]Ibid., p. 148.

[53]"The Enduring Chill," *The Complete Stories of Flannery O'Connor,* p. 376.

[54]"The Comforts of Home," *The Complete Stories of Flannery O'Connor,* p. 384.

[55]Ibid., p. 385.

[56]Ibid.

Chapter Three

[1]*Mystery and Manners*, p. 163.

[2]*The Presence of Grace and Other Book Reviews*, compiled by Leo J. Zuber, ed. Carter W. Martin (Athens: University of Georgia Press, 1983), p. 16.

[3]"Parker's Back," *The Complete Stories of Flannery O'Connor*, pp. 512-13.

[4]Ibid., p. 514.

[5]See "Anagogical Realism in Flannery O'Connor," *Renascence*, 37 (Winter 1985), 80-95 for a discussion of the convergence of sun, moon, and woods imagery in O'Connor's stories.

[6]"Parker's Back," *The Complete Stories of Flannery O'Connor*, p. 520.

[7]Ibid., p. 521.

[8]"The Fiction Writer and His Country," *Mystery and Manners*, p. 34.

[9]"The Lame Shall Enter First," *The Complete Stories of Flannery O'Connor*, p. 454.

[10]Ibid., p. 477.

[11]O'Connor underlined the following passage in J. Chaine's *God's Heralds: A Guide to the Prophets of Israel*, trans. Brendan McGrath (New York: Joseph F. Wagner, 1955), p. 123: "Ezechial receives an order to swallow a book full of lamentations in order that he may assimilate and then utter them to the children of Juda. In the Apocalypse (10:1-11) St. John also swallows a book. In the Orient there was an ancient custom of swallowing a book as a means of assimilating its power."

[12]"The Lame Shall Enter First," *The Complete Stories of Flannery O'Connor*, p. 462.

[13]Ibid., p. 481.

[14]Ibid., p. 461.

[15]*Flannery O'Connor: The Imagination of Extremity*, p. 79. After examining the manuscripts of the early versions of this story, Asals concludes that they reveal "O'Connor's primary commitment to the literal and the actual and her struggles to penetrate the world of matter, to discover within it the metaphorical resonance that would create the double vision" (p. 81).

[16]"The Artificial Nigger," *The Complete Stories of Flannery O'Connor*, p. 249.

[17]Ibid., p. 250.

[18]Ibid., pp. 249-50.

[19]Ibid., p. 251.

[20]Ibid., p. 259.

[21]Ibid., p. 257.

[22]Ibid., p. 250.

[23]Ibid., p. 266.

[24]Ibid., p. 267.

[25]See George Cheatham, "Jesus, O'Connor's Artificial Nigger," *Studies in Short Fiction*, 22 (Fall 1985), 479.

[26]"The Artificial Nigger," *The Complete Stories of Flannery O'Connor*, pp. 269-70.

[27]Ibid., p. 269.

[28]Ibid., p. 270.

[29]Ibid.

Chapter Four

[1]"Novelist and Believer," *Mystery and Manners*, p. 163.

[2]*Flannery O'Connor: The Imagination of Extremity,* p. 221. O'Connor marked the following passage in her personal copy of Justus George Lawler's *The Christian Imagination: Studies in Religious Thought* (Westminster, MD: Newman Press, 1955), p. 56: "Perhaps this rather delicate subject of sacramentalized nature, because it rests on so subtle a foundation, can be clarified by the following parallel: just as the gifts of the Holy Spirit must be present in a vague, passive manner in the soul before there can be true contemplation, so it is fitting that there be in matter, before it can be ennobled in the last day, a certain unactualized splendor which renders possible this future reception of excellence. Man, recognizing this disposition toward the perfection of its nature, treats matter with a view to its worth, in a manner analogous to that whereby Christians treat infidels with reverence because they are potentially members of the Mystical Body. Now it is this 'potency' in matter that is one reason for speaking of the sacramental aspect of nature."

[3]"The Displaced Person," *The Complete Stories of Flannery O'Connor,* p. 194.

[4]Ibid.

[5]*Shelley: Poetical Works,* ed. Thomas Hutchinson (London: Oxford University Press, 1905, reprinted 1967), p. 550.

[6]"The Displaced Person," *The Complete Stories of Flannery O'Connor,* p. 194.

[7]Ibid., p. 198.

[8]"Parker's Back," *The Complete Stories of Flannery O'Connor,* p. 515.

[9]"The Displaced Person," *The Complete Stories of Flannery O'Connor,* p. 196.

[10]Ibid., p. 205.

[11]Ibid.

[12]Ibid., p. 209.

[13]Ibid., p. 210.

[14]Ibid., p. 213.

[15]Ibid., p. 214.

[16]Ibid., p. 219.

[17]Ibid., p. 229.

[18]Ibid., p. 231.

[19]Ibid., p. 226.

[20]Ibid., p. 234.

[21]Ibid., p. 235.

[22]Alan W. Watts, *Myth and Ritual in Christianity* (New York: Grove Press, 1960), p. 200.

[23]"A Temple of the Holy Ghost," *The Complete Stories of Flannery O'Connor,* p. 236.

[24]Ibid., p. 237.

[25]Ibid., p. 240.

[26]Ibid., p. 238.

[27]In O'Connor's personal copy of Max Lackmann's *The Augsburg Confession and Catholic Unity,* trans. Walter R. Bouman (New York: Herder and Herder, 1963), she has marked the following passage in which Lackmann quotes Luther: ". . . the whole Scripture conveys these two teachings. One is the Law, which shows us our misery and punishes our sins. The other teaching is the Gospel; for God's promise, through which he offers us grace in Christ and in the

promise of grace, is repeated throughout the whole of Scripture, beginning with Adam," p. 78.

[28]"A Temple of the Holy Ghost," *The Complete Stories of Flannery O'Connor*, p. 237.

[29]Ibid., p. 242.

[30]Ibid.

[31]Ibid., p. 243.

[32]Ibid., p. 246.

[33]Ibid., pp. 247-48.

[34]Ibid., p. 248.

[35]Ibid.

[36]"The Enduring Chill," *The Complete Stories of Flannery O'Connor*, p. 362.

[37]Ibid., p. 374.

[38]Ibid., p. 381.

[39]Ibid., pp. 375-76.

[40]Ibid., p. 377.

[41]Ibid., p. 360.

[42]Ibid., p. 378.

[43]Ibid., p. 382.

[44]"The River," *The Complete Stories of Flannery O'Connor*, p. 174.

[45]Ibid., p. 162.

[46]Ibid., p. 163.

[47]David Jones, *Epoch and Artist* (London: Faber and Faber, 1959), p. 157.

[48]"Journey of the Magi," *The Complete Poems and Plays of T.S. Eliot* (London: Faber and Faber, 1969), p. 104.

[49]"The River," *The Complete Stories of Flannery O'Connor*, p. 165.

[50]Ibid., p. 168.

[51]*The Presence of Grace*, p. 77.

[52]"The River," *The Complete Stories of Flannery O'Connor*, p. 166.

[53]"Novelist and Believer," *Mystery and Manners*, p. 163.

[54]"The River," *The Complete Stories of Flannery O'Connor*, pp. 162-63.

[55]"Novelist and Believer," *Mystery and Manners*, p. 162.

[56]*The Habit of Being*, p. 171.

Chapter Five

[1]After reading *Wise Blood* one Unitarian woman in a book discussion group I was leading complained that she found the novel compelling, but that it was difficult to understand the kind of God O'Connor was revealing. The characters, this woman said, were so degenerate that they did not deserve grace, but they received it anyway. O'Connor would have been pleased, I believe.

[2]Charles Ruas, *Conversations with American Writers* (New York: Alfred A. Knopf, 1985), pp. 8-9.

[3]"A Good Man Is Hard to Find," *The Complete Stories of Flannery O'Connor*, p. 117.

[4]Ibid., p. 118.

[5]Ibid.

[6]Kathleen Feeley notes that in this story "Flannery O'Connor uses symbolic language to describe death as an entrance into an awareness of history." *Flannery O'Connor: Voice of the Peacock* (New Brunswick, NJ: Rutgers University Press, 1972), p. 93.

[7]"A Good Man Is Hard to Find," *The Complete Stories of Flannery O'Connor,* pp. 131-32.

[8]"The Misfit explains his philosophy clearly, and its echoes can be heard in the voices of Albert Camus, Martin Heidegger, and other alienated agnostics of our time. Because he 'wasn't there,' and he couldn't 'know,' he refused to open his mind to belief. Some writers might have made him an existential hero, but Flannery O'Connor portrays the moral sterility of his world." Kathleen Feeley, *Flannery O'Connor: Voice of the Peacock,* p. 73.

[9]"A Good Man Is Hard to Find," *The Complete Stories of Flannery O'Connor,* p. 133.

[10]"On Her Own Work," *Mystery and Manners,* pp. 110-11.

[11]*The Habit of Being,* pp. 186-90. See also John R. May, *The Pruning Word: The Parables of Flannery O'Connor* (IN: Notre Dame University Press, 1976), pp. 101-105. Professor May points out that "the conflict between Mark Fortune and Mary Fortune Pitts easily yields to allegorical interpretation" (p. 101).

[12]"A View of the Woods," *The Complete Stories of Flannery O'Connor,* p. 347.

[13]Ibid., p. 348.

[14]Ibid., p. 335.

[15]Ibid., p. 347.

[16]Ibid., p. 348.

[17]Ibid., p. 353.

[18]Ibid.

[19]Ibid., p. 356.

[20]Ibid., p. 341.

[21]Ibid., p. 356.

[22]"A Circle in the Fire," *The Complete Stories of Flannery O'Connor,* p. 176.

[23]Ibid., p. 179.

[24]Ibid., p. 180.

[25]Ibid., p. 186.

[26]Ibid., pp. 178-79.

[27]Ibid., p. 179.

[28]Ibid., p. 192.

[29]Ibid., p. 193.

[30]See John R. May, *The Pruning Word,* pp. 82-83 for a discussion of the parallels between the story and chapter three of the Book of Daniel.

[31]"A Circle in the Fire," *The Complete Stories of Flannery O'Connor,* p. 175.

[32]Ibid., p. 186.

[33]*The Habit of Being,* p. 438.

[34]*The Presence of Grace,* p. 108.

[35]Teilhard de Chardin, *The Phenomenon of Man* (New York: Harper and Row, 1959), p. 33.

[36]Ibid., p. 36.

[37]"Everything That Rises Must Converge," *The Complete Stories of Flannery O'Connor*, p. 405.

[38]Ibid., p. 408.

[39]Ibid., p. 419.

[40]Ibid., pp. 405-406.

[41]Ibid., p. 407.

[42]*The Phenomenon of Man*, p. 263.

[43]"Everything That Rises Must Converge," *The Habit of Being*, p. 420.

[44]For a perceptive explanation of the way in which O'Connor reads Teilhard de Chardin, see Gilbert H. Muller, *Nightmares and Visions: Flannery O'Connor and the Catholic Grotesque* (Athens: University of Georgia Press, 1972), pp. 69-71.

[45]*The Habit of Being*, p. 468.

[46]"Greenleaf," *The Complete Stories of Flannery O'Connor*, p. 311.

[47]Ibid., p. 315.

[48]Frederick Asals, "The Mythic Dimensions of Flannery O'Connor's 'Greenleaf,' " *Studies in Short Fiction*, 5, 317-330.

[49]"Greenleaf," *The Complete Stories of Flannery O'Connor*, p. 316.

[50]Ibid., p. 317.

[51]Ibid., p. 313.

[52]Ibid., p. 320.

[53]Ibid., p. 332.

[54]Ibid.

[55]Ibid., p. 333.

[56]Ibid.

[57]"Revelation," *The Complete Stories of Flannery O'Connor*, pp. 491-92.

[58]Ibid., p. 500.

[59]Ibid., p. 502.

[60]Ibid., p. 507.

[61]Ibid., p. 508.

[62]Andre Bleikasten, "The Heresy of Flannery O'Connor," *Critical Essays on Flannery O'Connor*, ed. Melvin J. Friedman and Beverly Lyon Clark (Boston: G.K. Hall, 1985), pp. 153, 156.

Chapter Six

[1]Flannery O'Connor, *Wise Blood* (New York: Farrar, Straus & Giroux, 1962).

[2]Martha Stephens, *The Question of Flannery O'Connor* (Baton Rouge: Louisiana State University Press, 1973), p. 49.

[3]*Flannery O'Connor: The Imagination of Extremity*, p. 41.

[4]Miles Orvell, *Invisible Parade: The Fiction of Flannery O'Connor* (Philadelphia: Temple University Press, 1972), p. 92.

[5]See *Literature in the Light of the Emblem*, pp. 172-74.

[6]*Wise Blood*, p. 22.

[7]Ibid.

[8]In *Flannery O'Connor: The Imagination of Extremity*, Frederick Asals feels the lack of these symbols indicates that O'Connor's vision in this novel is not sacramental. He says that instead of reflecting the Catholic sacramental view

of life, she is here doing what she described as the aim of modern fiction: "reflect[ing] our broken condition" (pp. 59-60). That O'Connor did not use her usual symbols here in this first novel is actually no proof that her vision is less than sacramental. The sacramental view would allow her to use any earthly object as a vehicle for God's grace. In *Wise Blood* the car, the mummy, the potato peeler, even Hazel's hat become objects capable of carrying God's truth.

[9]*Wise Blood*, pp. 117-20.

In "Paul, Francis, and Hazel Motes: Conversion at Taulkinham," *Thought*, vol. 59 (December 1984), p. 493, Richard Giannone has noted the transformation of this Old Testament cloud into the dove of the Gospels at the end of the seventh chapter of *Wise Blood*: "Hazel drives on the other way from the cloud into deeper degrees of blindness, from the ludicrous to the blasphemous. No matter. The cloud cleaves to him even as he denies the spirit. The glory of the cloud resides in its patient hovering. When the eye is ready to catch sight of it, the radiance will be there in saving visibility."

[10]*Wise Blood*, p. 9.

[11]Ibid., p. 122.

[12]Ibid., p. 170.

[13]Ibid., p. 55.

[14]Ibid., p. 16.

[15]Ibid., p. 20.

[16]Ibid., p. 70.

[17]Ibid., p. 73.

[18]Ibid., p. 113.

[19]Ibid., p. 50.

[20]Ibid., p. 30.

[21]Ibid., p. 34.

[22]Ibid., p. 53.

[23]Ibid., p. 225.

[24]*Flannery O'Connor: The Imagination of Extremity*, p. 41.

[25]*Wise Blood*, p. 214.

[26]Ibid., p. 91.

[27]Ibid., p. 224.

[28]Ibid., p. 53.

[29]*The Habit of Being*, p. 476. O'Connor marked the following passage in her copy of Karl Barth's *Evangelical Theology: An Introduction*, trans. Grover Foley (New York: Holt, Rinehart and Winston, 1963), p. 104: " 'I hear the message well enough, but what I lack is faith,' said Goethe's Faust. Yes, indeed—who does *not* lack faith? Who *can* believe? Certainly no one would believe if he maintained that he 'had' faith, so that nothing was lacking to him, and that he 'could' believe. Whoever believes, knows and confesses that he cannot 'by his own understanding and power' in any way believe. He will simply *perform* this believing, without losing sight of the unbelief that continually accompanies him and makes itself felt. Called and illumined by the Holy Spirit as he is, he does not understand himself; he cannot help but completely wonder at himself."

[30]*Wise Blood*, p. 9.
[31]Ibid., p. 10.
[32]Ibid., p. 37.
[33]Ibid., p. 43.
[34]Ibid., p. 50.
[35]Marshall Bruce Gentry, *Flannery O'Connor's Religion of the Grotesque* (Jackson: University Press of Mississippi, 1986), pp. 127-28. See also Rebecca Roxburgh Butler, "*Wise Blood*'s Joy in Contradiction," *The Flannery O'Connor Bulletin*, 10 (Autumn 1981), 23-28.
[36]*Wise Blood*, p. 122.
[37]Ibid., p. 140.
[38]Ibid., p. 141.
[39]Ibid.
[40]Ibid., p. 99.
[41]Ibid., p. 187.
[42]Marion Montgomery, *Why Flannery O'Connor Stayed Home* (LaSalle, IL: Sherwood Sugden and Co., 1981), p. 433.
[43]See *Literature in the Light of the Emblem*, pp. 104-106.
[44]*Wise Blood*, p. 189.
[45]Ibid., p. 165.
[46]Christian Metz, "Instant Self-Contradiction," *On Signs*, ed. Marshall Blonsky (Baltimore: The Johns Hopkins Press, 1985), p. 262.
[47]*Wise Blood*, p. 85.
[48]Ibid., p. 142.
[49]Ibid., p. 87.
[50]Ibid., p. 197.
[51]*Flannery O'Connor: The Imagination of Extremity*, p. 44.
[52]Ibid., p. 45. Asals goes on to call this ritualistic cleaning "the purification of the tabernacle preparatory to the entrance of his god. In keeping with the tenor of his religion, the washstand is adorned with images drawn from nature and surmounted with the wings of eagles rather than cherubim. Instead of a mercy seat there is a place for a slop-jar—a sly comment on the value of Enoch's worship—and it is here, he vaguely imagines, that 'rites and mysteries' will be performed" (pp. 45-46).
[53]*Wise Blood*, p. 132.
[54]John Bunyan, *The Pilgrim's Progress* (Grand Rapids, MI: Zondervan, 1967), pp. 32-33.
[55]*Wise Blood*, p. 133.
[56]Ibid., p. 132.
[57]*The Pilgrim's Progress*, p. 33.
[58]*Wise Blood*, p. 138.
[59]Ibid., p. 141.
[60]*The Pilgrim's Progress*, p. 39.
[61]Leon V. Driskell and Joan T. Brittain, *The Eternal Crossroads: The Art of Flannery O'Connor* (Lexington: University Press of Kentucky, 1971), p. 52.
[62]*Wise Blood*, p. 112.
[63]Ibid., p. 113.

[64]Ibid., p. 56.
[65]Ibid., p. 60.
[66]Ibid., p. 110.
[67]See Marshall Bruce Gentry, *Flannery O'Connor's Religion of the Grotesque*, pp. 126-27 for a discussion of the close identification of sex and redemption in *Wise Blood*.
[68]*Wise Blood*, p. 152.
[69]Ibid., p. 153.
[70]Ibid., p. 160.
[71]Ibid., p. 10.
[72]Again John Donne's poetry comes to mind. See, for example, "The Canonization," "The Legacie," "Love's Alchymie," "The Apparition," "The Relique," "The Dissolution," and others.
[73]*Wise Blood*, p. 203.
[74]Ibid., pp. 204-205.
[75]*Flannery O'Connor: Voice of the Peacock*, pp. 63-64.
[76]*Flannery O'Connor's Religion of the Grotesque*, p. 127.
[77]*Wise Blood*, p. 214.
[78]Ibid., p. 215.
[79]Ibid., p. 222.
[80]*The Habit of Being*, p. 354.
[81]*Wise Blood*, p. 216.
[82]"Paul, Francis, and Hazel Motes: Conversion at Taulkinham," *Thought*, pp. 484, 501-502.
[83]*The Habit of Being*, pp. 69-70.
[84]*Wise Blood*, p. 232.

Chapter Seven
[1]*The Question of Flannery O'Connor*, p. 124.
[2]Robert Coles, *Flannery O'Connor's South* (Baton Rouge: Louisiana State University Press, 1980), p. 144.
[3]*Flannery O'Connor's Religion of the Grotesque*, p. 150.
[4]As reported by Joel Wells, "Off the Cuff," *The Critic*, 21 (August-September 1962), 4-5. Reprinted in *Conversations with Flannery O'Connor*, ed. Rosemary M. Magee (Jackson: University Press of Mississippi, 1987), p. 88.
[5]*The Pruning Word*, p. 150.
[6]John A. Hardon, S.J. *The Catholic Catechism* (Garden City, NY: Doubleday, 1975), p. 511.
[7]Flannery O'Connor, *The Violent Bear It Away* (New York: Farrar, Straus & Giroux, 1962), p. 6.
[8]Ibid., p. 126.
[9]Ibid., p. 54.
[10]Ibid., p. 23.
[11]Ibid., p. 194.
[12]Ibid., p. 56.
[13]Ibid., p. 9.
[14]Ibid., p. 62.

[15]Ibid., p. 10.

[16]Ibid., p. 209.

[17]In *The Catholic Catechism*, p. 505, John Hardon says, "Through the symbolic action of washing with water and the use of appropriate ritual words, the baptized person is cleansed of all his sins and incorporated into Christ."

[18]*The Violent Bear It Away*, p. 19.

[19]Ibid., p. 131.

[20]Ibid., p. 132.

[21]*The Catholic Catechism*, p. 32. O'Connor marked the following sentence in her copy of Karl Barth's *Evangelical Theology: An Introduction*, trans. Grover Foley (New York: Holt, Rinehart and Winston, 1963), p. 48: "It is a terrible thing when God keeps silence, and by keeping silence speaks."

[22]*The Violent Bear It Away*, pp. 166-67.

[23]Ibid., p. 174.

[24]Ibid., p. 171.

[25]See *Nightmares and Visions*, p. 65.

[26]*The Violent Bear It Away*, p. 161.

[27]Ibid., p. 216.

[28]Ibid., p. 39.

[29]Ibid., p. 50.

[30]Ibid., p. 166.

[31]Ibid., p. 58.

[32]In her copy of Robert A. Caponigri's *Modern Catholic Thinkers: An Anthology* (New York: Harper and Brothers, 1960), p. 38, O'Connor marked the following passage with an "S" sign: "But in our struggle and wanderings in search of our one Love and of ourselves we are at the mercy of a disordered imagination, heady passions and unruly impulses, and we are at the mercy of the cunning stranger, the congenial and the novel." (As reported by Arthur Kinney, *Flannery O'Connor's Library*, p. 35).

[33]*The Violent Bear It Away*, p. 19.

[34]In *Flannery O'Connor: Voice of the Peacock*, Kathleen Feeley notes that "Tarwater initially fails to understand the meaning of 'freedom in the Lord.' For instance, when his great-uncle takes him to the city on legal business, Tarwater is scandalized that the old man ignores what Tarwater thinks is the evident evil around him. When the prophet fails to thunder out denunciations of the city, Tarwater demands: 'What kind of a prophet are you?' The old man tells him 'mildly' that he is in town on business and dismisses his protests with 'And I know what times I'm called and what times I ain't.' He is truly free in the Lord." See also Dorothy Tuck McFarland, *Flannery O'Connor* (New York: Frederick Ungar, 1976), p. 108ff. for a discussion of the problem of freedom in the novel.

[35]*Flannery O'Connor: The Imagination of Extremity*, pp. 181-82.

[36]*The Habit of Being*, p. 382.

[37]This consideration of the law seems related to the Calvinist work ethic which "if followed as the only road to material and spiritual success, leads inexorably to destruction." Shannon Burns, "Flannery O'Connor: The Work Ethic," *The Flannery O'Connor Bulletin*, 8 (Autumn 1979), p. 55.

[38]*The Violent Bear It Away*, p. 46.

[39]Ibid., p. 30.

[40]Ibid., pp. 74-75.

[41]In a panel discussion about O'Connor at Georgia College, Robert Drake quoted the first few lines of Hopkins' sonnet, "God's Grandeur," and said, "Man has done everything he can to soil and smear and sear and bend the world from God, but it's still this green world of God's. That is the other side of the coin which a lot of critics who misread, I think, neglect. God is still in charge in her world and it is still this green world of God's, and she never allows you to forget it." *The Flannery O'Connor Bulletin*, 3 (Autumn 1974), p. 66.

[42]Albert Sonnenfeld, "Flannery O'Connor: The Catholic Writer as Baptist," *Critical Essays on Flannery O'Connor*, pp. 116-17.

[43]*The Violent Bear It Away*, p. 169.

[44]Ibid., pp. 51-52.

[45]Ibid., p. 232.

[46]Ibid., p. 7.

[47]Ibid., p. 42.

[48]Ibid., p. 49.

[49]Ibid., p. 42.

[50]Ibid., p. 236.

[51]Ibid., p. 237.

[52]In *Flannery O'Connor: The Imagination of Extremity*, p. 170, Asals writes extensively on the motif of the double in O'Connor's work and observes that "at its furthest reaches the elaborately conceived double motif extends into all aspects of *The Violent Bear It Away* to become one of its major unifying devices . . . . This doubling becomes incarnated in language and action to set up recurrent echoes which force the mind backward and forward over the entire range of the book."

[53]*The Violent Bear It Away*, p. 8.

[54]Ibid., p. 15.

[55]Ibid., p. 77.

[56]Ibid., p. 48.

[57]Ibid., p. 240.

[58]*The Catholic Catechism*, p. 504.

[59]*The Violent Bear It Away*, p. 113.

[60]Ibid., pp. 113-14.

[61]*Flannery O'Connor: The Imagination of Extremity*, p. 177.

[62]*The Violent Bear It Away*, p. 80.

[63]Ibid.

[64]*Invisible Parade*, p. 111.

[65]*Flannery O'Connor: Voice of the Peacock*, p. 161.

[66]*The Violent Bear It Away*, p. 241.

[67]Ibid., p. 242.

[68]Ibid., p. 202.

[69]Ibid., p. 242.

Chapter Eight

[1]"Introduction," *The Complete Stories of Flannery O'Connor*, p. xvi.

[2]*The Habit of Being*, pp. 579-80.

[3]Ibid., p. 585.

[4]Ibid., p. 587.

[5]Ibid., p. 588.

[6]Ibid., p. 593.

[7]Although we come to different conclusions, Ralph C. Wood has also observed that "Judgement Day" seems to represent a new direction for O'Connor. "From Fashionable Tolerance to Unfashionable Redemption: A Reading of Flannery O'Connor's First and Last Stories," *The Flannery O'Connor Bulletin* 7 (Autumn 1978), pp. 10-25.

[8]Terry Eagleton, *Literary Theory* (Minneapolis: University of Minnesota Press, 1983), p. 129.

[9]"Judgement Day," *The Complete Stories of Flannery O'Connor*, p. 531.

[10]Ibid.

[11]*Literary Theory*, p. 140.

[12]"Judgement Day," *The Complete Stories of Flannery O'Connor*, p. 542.

[13]Ibid., p. 532.

[14]Ibid., p. 537.

[15]Ibid., p. 538.

[16]Julia Kristeva, "The Speaking Subject," *On Signs*, p. 212, n. 3.

[17]"Judgement Day," *The Complete Stories of Flannery O'Connor*, p. 545.

[18]Ibid., p. 533.

[19]Ibid., p. 540.

[20]Ibid., p. 541.

[21]Ibid., p. 548.

[22]Ibid., p. 543.

[23]Ibid., p. 549.

[24]*The Habit of Being*, p. 342.

[25]"On Her Own Work," *Mystery and Manners*, p. 114.

Bibliography

Abbot, Louise. "Remembering Flannery O'Connor." *The Southern Literary Journal*, 2 (Spring 1970): 3-25.

The Added Dimension: The Art and Mind of Flannery O'Connor, ed. Melvin J. Friedman and Lewis A. Lawson. New York: Fordham University Press, 1966.

Alpaugh, David J. "Emblem and Interpretation in The Pilgrim's Progress." *English Literary History*, 33 (1966), 200-314.

Asals, Frederick. *Flannery O'Connor: The Imagination of Extremity*. Athens: University of Georgia Press, 1982.

————. "The Mythic Dimensions of Flannery O'Connor's 'Greenleaf.' " *Studies in Short Fiction*, 5, 317-330.

Barth, Karl. *Evangelical Theology: An Introduction*, trans. Grover Foley. New York: Holt, Rinehart and Winston, 1963.

Bleikestan, Andre. "The Heresy of Flannery O'Connor." *Critical Essays on Flannery O'Connor*, ed. Melvin J. Friedman and Beverly Lyon Clark. Boston: G. K. Hall, 1985.

Browning, Preston M., Jr. *Flannery O'Connor*. Carbondale and Edwardsville: Southern Illinois University Press, 1974.

Bryant, J.A. "Shakespeare's Allegory: The Winter's Tale." *The Sewanee Review*, 63 (Spring 1955): 202-222.

Bunyan, John. *The Pilgrim's Progress*. Grand Rapids: Zondervan, 1967.

Burns, Shannon. "Flannery O'Connor: The Work Ethic." *The Flannery O'Connor Bulletin*, 8 (Autumn 1979): 54-67.

Burns, Stuart L. " 'Torn By the Lord's Eye': Flannery O'Connor's Use of Sun Imagery." *Twentieth Century Literature*, 13 (1967): 154-166.

Butler, Rebecca Roxburgh. "*Wise Blood*'s Joy in Contradiction." *The Flannery O'Connor Bulletin*, 10 (Autumn, 1981), 23-28.

Caponigri, Robert A. *Modern Catholic Thinkers: An Anthology.* New York: Harper and Brothers, 1960.

Chaines, J. *God's Heralds: A Guide to the Prophets of Israel,* trans. Brendan McGrath. New York: Joseph F. Wagner, 1955.

Cheatham, George. "Jesus, O'Connor's Artificial Nigger." *Studies in Short Fiction,* 22 (Fall 1985), 475-479.

Coles, Robert. *Flannery O'Connor's South.* Baton Rouge: Louisiana State University Press, 1980.

Critical Essays on Flannery O'Connor, ed. Melvin J. Friedman and Beverly Lyon Clark. Boston: G. K. Hall and Co., 1985.

Daly, Peter. *Literature in the Light of the Emblem.* Toronto: University of Toronto Press, 1979.

Desmond, John F. "Risen Sons: History, Consciousness, and Personality in the Fiction of Flannery O'Connor." *Thought,* 59 (Dec. 1984), 462-482.

Driskell, Leon V. and Joan T. Brittain. *The Eternal Crossroads: The Art of Flannery O'Connor.* Lexington: University Press of Kentucky, 1971.

Eagleton, Terry. *Literary Theory.* Minneapolis: University of Minnesota Press, 1983.

Eggenschwiler, David. *The Christian Humanism of Flannery O'Connor.* Detroit: Wayne State University Press, 1972.

Eliot. T. S. *The Complete Poems and Plays.* London: Faber and Faber, 1969.

Feeley, Kathleen. *Flannery O'Connor: Voice of the Peacock.* New Brunswick, NJ: Rutgers University Press, 1972.

Ferguson, George. *Signs and Symbols in Christian Art.* New York: Oxford University Press, 1954.

Freeman, Rosemary. *English Emblem Books,* 1948. Reprinted New York: Octagon Books, 1966.

Gentry, Marshall Bruce. *Flannery O'Connor's Religion of the Grotesque.* Jackson: University Press of Mississippi, 1986.

Getz, Lorine M. *Nature and Grace in Flannery O'Connor's Fiction.* New York: The Edwin Mellen Press, 1982.

Giannone, Richard. "Paul, Francis, and Hazel Motes: Conversion at Taulkinham." *Thought,* 59 (December 1984), 483-503.

Hardon, John A., S. J. *The Catholic Catechism.* Garden City, NY: Doubleday, 1975.

Hawkes, John. "Flannery O'Connor's Devil." *Critical Essays on Flannery O'Connor,* ed. Melvin J. Friedman and Beverly Lyon Clark. Boston: G. K. Hall, 1985. Reprinted from *The Sewanee Review,* 70 (1962), 395-407.

Hendin, Josephine. *The World of Flannery O'Connor.* Bloomington: Indiana University Press, 1970.

James, William. *The Varieties of Religious Experience: A Study in Human Nature.* New York: Crowell-Collier, 1961.

Jones, David. *Epoch and Artist.* London: Faber and Faber, 1959.

Kessler, Edward. *Flannery O'Connor and the Language of Apocalypse.* Princeton University Press, 1986.

Kinney, Arthur. *Flannery O'Connor's Library: Resources of Being.* Athens: University of Georgia Press, 1985.

Kristeva, Julia. "The Speaking Subject." *On Signs,* ed. Marshall Blonsky. Baltimore: The Johns Hopkins University Press, 1985.

Lackmann, Max. *The Augsburg Confession and Catholic Unity,* trans. Walter R. Bouman. New York: Herder and Herder, 1963.

Lawler, Justus George. *The Christian Imagination: Studies in Religious Thought.* Westminster, MD: Newman Press, 1955.

Linehan, Thomas M. "Anagogical Realism in Flannery O'Connor." *Renascence,* 37 (Winter 1985), 80-95.

May, John R. *The Pruning Word: The Parables of Flannery O'Connor.* Notre Dame: University of Notre Dame Press, 1976.

McFarland, Dorothy Tuck. *Flannery O'Connor.* New York: Frederick Ungar, 1976.

Metz, Christian. "Instant Self-Contradiction," *On Signs,* ed. Marshall Blonsky. Baltimore: The Johns Hopkins Press, 1985.

Montgomery, Marion. *Why Flannery O'Connor Stayed Home.* La Salle, IL: Sherwood Sugden and Co., 1981.

Muller, Gilbert H. *Nightmares and Visions: Flannery O'Connor and the Catholic Grotesque.* Athens: University of Georgia Press, 1972.

O'Connor, Flannery. *The Complete Stories.* New York: Farrar, Straus and Giroux, 1962.

———. *Conversations with Flannery O'Connor,* ed. Rosemary M. Magee. Jackson: University Press of Mississippi, 1987.

———. *The Correspondence of Flannery O'Connor and the Brainard Cheneys,* ed. C. Ralph Stephens. Jackson: University Press of Mississippi, 1986.

———. *The Habit of Being: The Letters of Flannery O'Connor,* ed. Sally Fitzgerald. New York: Farrar, Straus and Giroux, 1979.

———. *Mystery and Manners,* eds. Sally and Robert Fitzgerald. New York: Farrar, Straus and Giroux, 1969.

———. *The Presence of Grace and Other Book Reviews,* compiled by Leo J. Zuber, ed. Carter W. Martin. Athens: University of Georgia Press, 1983.

———. *The Violent Bear It Away.* New York: Farrar, Straus and Giroux, 1960.

———. *Wise Blood.* New York: Farrar, Straus and Giroux, 1962.

Orvell, Miles. *Invisible Parade: The Fiction of Flannery O'Connor.* Philadelphia: Temple University Press, 1972.

Praz, Mario. *The Flaming Heart: Essays on Crashaw, Machiavelli and Other Studies in the Relations Between Italian and English Literature from Chaucer to T. S. Eliot.* New York: Doubleday, 1958.

Quilligan, Maureen. *The Language of Allegory: Defining the Genre.* Ithaca: Cornell University Press, 1979.

Ruas, Charles. *Conversations with American Writers.* New York: Alfred A. Knopf, 1985.

Sanders, Andrea. "'Mirrors Arranged in a Circle Around One Center': The O'Connor Mystery Cycle." *Postscript,* 2 (1985): 1-9.

Sonnenfield, Albert. "Flannery O'Connor: The Catholic Writer as Baptist." *Critical Essays on Flannery O'Connor,* ed. Melvin J. Friedman and Beverly Lyon Clark. Boston: G. K. Hall and Co., 1985.

Stephens, Martha. *The Question of Flannery O'Connor.* Baton Rouge: Louisiana State University, 1982.

Teilhard de Chardin. *The Phenomenon of Man.* New York: Harper and Row, 1959.

Ulanov, Barry. *Sources and Resources: The Literary Tradition of Christian Humanism.* Westminster, MD: Newman Press, 1960.

Watts, Alan W. *Myth and Ritual in Christianity.* New York: Grove Press, 1960.

Westling, Louise. *Sacred Groves and Ravaged Gardens: The Fictions of Eudora Welty, Carson McCullers, and Flannery O'Connor.* Athens: University of Georgia Press, 1985.

Wood, Ralph. "From Fashionable Tolerance to Unfashionable Redemption: A Reading of Flannery O'Connor's First and Last Stories." *The Flannery O'Connor Bulletin,* 7 (Autumn, 1978), 10-25.

INDEX